Sharon Vanderlip, DVM

Hedgehogs

Everything About Purchase,
Care, and Nutrition

BARRON'S

CONTENTS

INTRODUCTION

Hedgehogs are extraordinary animals. Bright eyed, curious, and covered with quills, these charming little creatures can make delightful and unusual pets. Hedgehogs have unique behaviors, abilities, adaptations, and personalities. They also require special care and handling. If you have fallen under the spell of these sweet-faced, prickly pets, this book will take you on a fascinating journey into the secret life of one of the world's oldest, most primitive, and interesting animals. It will help you decide if an African pygmy hedgehog is the perfect pet for you and teach you how to properly care for one. So, read on! The diminutive and mysterious African pygmy hedgehog has a big story to tell!

What Is a Hedgehog?

The hedgehog is a small, spiny mammal native to Central Africa. It is best recognized for its thousands of short quills (2,000 to 3,500 on a baby, 5,000 to 7,000 on an adult) and for its appealing face.

Hedgehogs are not domestic animals. They are *wild* animals that may be *domestically raised* in captivity and may be tamed.

In the wild, the hedgehog's natural habitats include grasslands, savannahs, and scrub areas covering a very large geographical area ranging from Senegal on the western coast of the continent, all the way east to Sudan, and extending south as far as Zambia.

African pygmy hedgehogs are not really pygmies, miniatures, or dwarfs. They are not a variety or a breed. They are a true and distinct species. The word *pygmy* is simply used to denote the fact that the African pygmy

Important Note

There are 16 different species of hedgehogs. This book is about the care of African pygmy hedgehogs, the species most commonly kept as pets. Throughout the book, when we refer to "hedgehogs," we are referring to African pygmy hedgehogs.

Differences Between Hedgehogs and Other Mammals with Spines

Hedgehogs	Porcupines	Echidnas (spiny anteaters)	Egyptian Spiny Mice
Primitive placental mammals: *Erinaceomorpha* order	Large placental rodents: *Rodentia* order, *Caviomorpha* suborder	Primitive egg-laying mammals: *Monotremata* order	Small placental rodents: *Rodentia* order
Quills are short, mostly hollow, grooved, not barbed, securely attached in the skin, and do not lodge in attackers.	Quills are long and rigid, with a spongy interior. Some quills have microscopic barbs on the tips. Quills are easily released from the skin and lodge in attackers, causing intense pain as they migrate through body tissues. Porcupines cannot "shoot their quills."	Quills are not barbed and are not released into attacking predators.	Stiff, bristly-appearing fur resembles spines and makes it difficult for predators to swallow the mice.

hedgehog is smaller than its close hedgehog relatives. African pygmy hedgehogs are not related to other mammalian species that also have quills or spines, such as porcupines, echidnas (spiny anteaters), or spiny mice.

There are 16 extant (currently existing) species of hedgehogs, and although they may appear similar, they differ from each other in many ways. The African pygmy hedgehog is the species most commonly kept as a pet.

African Pygmy Hedgehog Characteristics

The African pygmy hedgehog is an attractive animal and an entertaining pet. Its scientific genus name, *Atelerix*, translates as "ineffective fighter." Its species name, *albiventris*, is Latin for "white belly" (*albi* meaning "white" and *ventris* meaning "abdomen"), in reference to the animal's white (or ivory or cream colored) fur on its underside. Combined, *Atelerix albiventris* means "ineffective fighter with a white belly." Hedgehogs assume a defensive position by rolling into a ball when threatened.

Other descriptive names for the African pygmy hedgehog include the *spiny hedgehog*, the *African hedgehog*, the *West African hedgehog*, and the *four-toed hedgehog*. Unlike other hedgehog species, the African pygmy hedgehog usually lacks, or has a reduced, big toe (hallux) on the hind feet.

Face: The foreface (muzzle, snout) is furred and moderately long. Muzzle color usually corresponds to the overall color of the quills. Hedgehogs with dark quills usually have dark muzzles and masks. Hedgehogs with light-colored quills usually have light-colored muzzles. The fur on the face, limbs, and underbelly of the animal is light colored (white, off-white, ivory, or cream colored) and soft.

Eyes: Hedgehogs have well-developed, medium-sized eyes placed on the sides of the head, approximately mid-distance between the ears and the nose. The eyes sit in a shallow socket. Eye color varies, depending on pigmentation and color variety. Eyes can be brown, dark brown, red, or, in the case of albinos, pink because of a lack of pigmentation. Hedgehogs appear to have poor vision and cannot judge vertical heights. They can easily fall from tables and countertops. Hedgehogs probably see only in shades of black, white, and gray.

Ears: The ears are small, rounded, short, and sparsely-haired. Hearing is very keen and is important in foraging for live food, such as insects. Hedgehogs are very sensitive to sounds.

Nose: The nose is broad, fleshy, sensitive, blunt, and hairless. The nose is usually pigmented and dark, except in albinos, in which case the nose is pink because of a lack of pigmentation.

Mouth: The mouth is small. It is difficult to see the teeth, except for the front incisors.

Whiskers (vibrissae): Hedgehogs have long whiskers that help them navigate by sense of touch during their nighttime activities. They also have tiny, almost inconspicuous microvibrissae (micro-whiskers) *under* the rhinarium (the hairless, moist areas around the nostrils). The microvibrissae are much more sensitive than the larger whiskers on the face and play an important role in food discrimination.

Body: The body is robust and compact. The underside of the body is furred. When running, the hedgehog's legs are visible and the abdomen

is raised off the ground. Hedgehogs are flexible and can easily bend sideways or curl into a tight ball. Hedgehogs can remain curled in a ball for long periods of time.

Mammary glands: Female hedgehogs generally have five pairs of mammary glands on their underside (varies from two to five pair).

Limbs: The limbs are slender and furred. The lower leg bones (tibia and fibula) are fused and give the delicate legs additional strength, but the limbs can easily break if stepped upon or trapped in wire.

Hedgehogs are good climbers. If the hedgehog is not overweight, the forelimbs are strong enough to enable the animal to pull up its full body weight to climb. Hedgehogs can also swim.

Feet: There are five toes on the front feet. The hind feet have four toes. They lack a hallux (big toe), or, in some cases, this toe is very small. For this reason, the African pygmy hedgehog was given its common name: *four-toed hedgehog*.

The feet and toes are well padded. The toes have nails. The second nail of the hind feet is naturally longer than the other nails. The toe-nails require regular trimming.

Gait: Hedgehogs walk on the soles of their feet (plantigrade) and have a rolling waddle when they walk. Hedgehogs are capable of sur-prising bursts of speed.

Tail: The tail is short, sparsely haired, and measures 1 to 2 inches (2.5–5 cm) in length. It is tucked under the animal and often not visible.

Quills: Quills are modified guard hairs that are thicker and stiffer than hair. The hedgehog's quills are smooth and short, measuring approxi-mately ¼ to 1 inch (0.5–2.5 cm) in length.

—————— **TIP** ——————

Teeth

African pygmy hedgehogs normally have 34 to 36 teeth. Their dental formula is:

i 3/2   c 1/1   p 2*/2   m 3/3

The number left of the slash represents one-half of the upper jaw (left or right side) and the number right of the slash represents one-half of the bottom jaw (left or right side).

i = incisors

There are six upper incisors and four lower incisors. The first incisors, located most centrally in the front of the mouth, are larger than the other incisors and are the most visible teeth upon examination. The upper third incisors have a double root.

c = canine teeth

The upper canine teeth have a double root.

p = premolars* In most African pygmy hedgehogs, the upper third premolar is reduced or absent. The second premolar may be missing.

m = molars

Dental problems and abnormalities, including missing and misaligned teeth, are common in African pygmy hedgehogs. A slight overbite is normal.

The tip of the quill is solid and slightly bent. The body of the quill consists of a rigid outer layer (cortex) and an inner medulla that is filled with air-space chambers separated by thin hori-zontal plates (struts), keeping the quill light-weight. Each quill is firmly attached in the skin, where it expands into a bulb, making it difficult to dislodge. Each quill can be raised by specialized erector muscles to which they are attached. Hedgehogs can raise some areas of quills independently of other areas. The quills on the brow can be raised independently from the quills on the back.

The African pygmy hedgehog's back is covered with quills, beginning at the brow or crown of the head, just in front of the ears and extending down the entire back and down the sides of the animal's body. There is a distinct, narrow parting tract on the middle of the head where quills are lacking. In newborn hedgehogs this parting can be easily identified to run the entire length of the body, from between the brows, over the back, to the rump. This tract is normal and should not be mistaken for quill loss or injury. It corresponds to the embryological development of the *orbicularis* musculature.

When a hedgehog is relaxed, its quills lie relatively flat on its body, pointing backward. When the animal is startled, it rolls into a ball and raises and crisscrosses its quills to deter predators.

Color: Quills may be banded or unbanded. Banded quills range from white to ivory or yellowish, with a central colored band that may range from shades of buff, apricot, cinnamon, light brown, and golden brown, to brown, dark brown, gray, or black. There may be a thinner

band above and below the central band. This thinner band is lighter in color than the wider central band. Quills are usually lighter at the base than at the tip, but variations exist. Unbanded quills are light colored with no central darker color band. Some unbanded quills have a color spot in the center of the quill.

African Pygmy Hedgehog Average Adult Measurements

Weight	Length of Head and Body	Length of Tail
Adult male: 16 oz.–21 oz. (448–588 g) Adult female: 8 oz.–18 oz. (224–504 g) Note: Weights vary among individuals. Average range is about 1 lb. or 448 g for an adult. African pygmy hedgehogs weighing more than 17.5 oz. (500 g) may be overweight.	5–12 inches (12.5–30 cm)	½ to 1½ inches (1.25–4 cm)

African Pygmy Hedgehog Facts

Origin	Central Africa from Sudan, to Senegal, to Zambia
Natural habitat	Grasslands, savannahs, and scrub areas
Natural predators in the wild	Jackals, wild dogs, ratels (honey badger *Mellivora capensis*), Verreaux's Eagle-owl (*Bubo lacteus*)
Diet in the wild	Omnivorous. Eats a wide variety of foods, including insects, slugs, worms, plants, fruits, lizards, frogs, mice, eggs, fungi, vegetation, and carrion.
Activity	Nocturnal (active at night), and crepuscular (*most* active during dusk and dawn). "Crepuscular" (from the French word *crépuscule*, meaning "twilight").
Recommended housing temperature	75°–85°F (24°–29°C) At temperatures below 65°F (18°C) or above 90°F (32°C), hedgehogs become stressed and lethargic. Temperature extremes cause death.
Humidity	55% or less. Hedgehogs are desert animals and do not tolerate high humidity well.
Lifestyle	Solitary
Hiding and sleeping places	Under leaves, under rock ledges, in logs, tree roots, crevices, shrubs, and holes
Illness	Multiple illnesses; the most common are numerous types of cancer, fatty liver disease, dental and gum disease, and skin problems.
Body temperature (rectal)	Normal body temperature is low compared with most small mammals—95°F (35°C) to 99°F (38°C).
Sensitivity to cold	At temperatures below 65°F (18°C), the hedgehog becomes lethargic. As the temperature drops, the animal may hibernate. It is dangerous to expose pet African pygmy hedgehogs to temperature extremes, or to allow them to hibernate.
Sensitivity to heat	At temperatures above 85°F (29°C) hedgehogs suffer from heat stress. African pygmy hedgehogs are very sensitive to heat and can quickly die from heatstroke.
Color	African pygmy hedgehogs are available in a wide variety of colors and patterns.
Life span	Average 3 to 6 years in captivity

The overall coloration of a hedgehog is determined by the colors of the bands or spots on the quills, the width of the bands, and the number and color of unbanded quills. African pygmy hedgehogs vary in color and patterns, from albino (complete lack of pigmentation), to light brown, to almost black. The more common color is called the *wild type*, or *agouti*. Agouti is a camouflage coloration pattern common among many animals of prey. The agouti color pattern and gene are named after the agouti, a large South American rodent with hairs of various bands of color along the shaft that give it a stippled, or ticked, appearance. Hedgehogs with the agouti pattern have quills that are light colored (usually off-white or ivory) at the base and tip and banded with various shades of brown, gray, or black.

Through selective breeding, hedgehog fanciers have produced animals in a wide variety of colors, shades, and patterns. Hedgehog color genetics and inheritance have not been completely mapped out, but hedgehog breeders continue to make progress in this fascinating and complicated area of study.

Hedgehog coloration is influenced by the animal's genetics, age, health, nutrition, and environment. African pygmy hedgehogs can change colors and patterns as they grow up and mature or lose and re-grow quills. Some hedgehogs fade in color as they age.

The hedgehog's quills serve multiple purposes:

1. Effective shock absorber to protect the animal from falls

2. Passive protection against predator attacks

3. Offensive action against other animals (head butting)

4. Camouflage coloration to blend in with natural environment and hide from predators

Brain: Hedgehogs are primitive animals with relatively primitive brains. The cerebral hemispheres of the hedgehog's brain are smooth, without elaboration or convolutions (folds). Convolutions in the brain allow for greater surface area. There is a direct correlation between intelligence and brain convolutions. In other words, African pygmy hedgehogs are not highly intelligent. But let's not underestimate this amazing little animal! Hedgehogs have existed for millennia while other species have come and gone extinct. The African pygmy hedgehog is a survivor that deserves our admiration and respect!

The Hedgehog's Place in Nature

Hedgehogs used to be classified as insectivores. Although insects are part of the hedgehog's natural diet, hedgehogs eat many other things as well. Hedgehogs eat plant and animal protein, so they are actually omnivorous. The order *Insectivora* is now defunct. It has been redefined, reclassified, and renamed—for many good reasons.

Insectivores have always been a challenge for taxonomists and a subject of lively debate among scientists. Insectivores were described as a primitive group of mammals that has remained unchanged throughout most of their evolution. Historically, the order *Insectivora* has been a catchall for many animals that did not fit within any other classification. Many small, primitive, insect-eating mammals were lumped together in the *Insectivora* order for more than a century, because scientists were not certain of their evolution or ancestry and did not know where else, or how else, to categorize them. Taxonomically (science of classification) and phylogenetically (method of determining relatedness among species based on genetic sequencing), the order *Insectivora* has been the least stable mammalian group. After extensive research, scientists have replaced the order *Insectivora* with two orders: *Erinaceomorpha* and *Soricomorpha*. Hedgehogs are in the order *Erinaceomorpha* and are no longer lumped together with the *Soricidae* (shrews), *Talpidae* (moles), and *Solenodontidae* (solenodons). These latter three families are now in the order *Soricomorpha*. Genetic sequencing has supported the phylogenetic relationships of this new classification.

African Pygmy Hedgehog Taxonomy

Kingdom *Animalia* (Animal Kingdom)
Phylum *Chordata* (animals having spinal columns)
Subphylum *Vertebrata* (vertebrates)
Class *Mammalia* (mammals: animals that nourish their young with milk from mammary glands)
Subclass *Theria* (mammals that give birth to live young, not in a shelled egg)
Infraclass *Eutheria* (placental mammals)
Order *Erinaceomorpha* (The Order *Insectivora* [insect eaters] has been replaced by 2 Orders: *Erinaceomorpha* and *Soricomorpha*.)
Family *Erinaceidae* (hedgehogs and gymnures)
Subfamily *Erinaceinae* (5 genera and 16 species of hedgehogs)
Genus *Atelerix* (4 species of African hedgehogs)
Species *Albiventris* (the African Pygmy Hedgehog)

Tenrecs and golden moles were once considered to be closely related to hedgehogs. New scientific evidence based on genetic studies (gene sequencing) suggests tenrecs and golden moles belong to a separate African clade of mammals, placing tenrecs and golden moles in a separate order, *Afrosoricida*, together with hyrax, elephant shrews, and the aardvark!

Hedgehog Classification

Animals, insects, and plants are classified and grouped according to their differences and similarities. Names are assigned according to kingdom, phylum, class, order, family, genus, and species. With each progressive category, animals grouped together are more closely related. The name given to a class, order, family, genus, or species may come from different sources. Animals can be named according to a special characteristic of their group, after the person who discovered them, or even after the geographical area they naturally inhabit.

Order Erinaceomorpha: Five Genera and 16 Species* of Hedgehogs

Erinaceomorpha
  Erinaceidae
    Erinaceinae
      Atelerix
        Atelerix albiventris: African pygmy hedgehog
        Atelerix algirus: Algerian or North African hedgehog
          Subspecies: *Atlerix algirus algirus*
          Subspecies: *Atelerix algirus girbanens*
          Subspecies: *Atelerix algirus vagans*
        Atelerix frontalis: South African hedgehog
          Subspecies: *Atelerix frontalis frontalis*
          Subspecies: *Atelerix frontalis angolae*
        Atelerix sclateri: Somali hedgehog
      Erinaceus
        Erinaceus amurensis: Amur hedgehog
        Erinaceus concolor: Southern White-Breasted hedgehog
        Erinaceus europaeus: West European hedgehog
        Erinaceus roumanicus: Northern White-Breasted hedgehog
      Hemiechinus
        Hemiechinus auritus: Long-eared hedgehog
        Hemiechinus collaris: Indian Long-eared hedgehog
      Mesechinus
        Mesechinus dauuricus: Daurian hedgehog
        Mesechinus hughi: Central Chinese, or Hugh's, hedgehog
      Paraechinus
        Paraechinus aethiopicus: Desert hedgehog
        Paraechinus hypomelas: Brandt's hedgehog
        Paraechinus micropus: Indian hedgehog
        Paraechinus nudiventris: Bare-bellied, Madras, hedgehog

*There are several *subspecies* of hedgehogs. For brevity, only the subspecies of *Atelerix* are listed in this chart.

Legend and Lore

Hedgehogs are mysterious creatures. It's not surprising that these remarkable nighttime animals, with their intriguing behaviors and curious appearance, have captured people's attention and imagination throughout the centuries. Misunderstood and sometimes maligned, they have inspired numerous legends and myths. Even Shakespeare (1564–1616) referred to hedgehogs in some of his plays, calling them urchins or hedge-pigs. In Shakespeare's *Macbeth*, Act 4, Scene 1, just before the famous "Double, double, toil and trouble" line, the second of the three witches says, "Thrice and once the hedge-pig whined." Scientists reported in a study that during courtship the male European hedgehog makes three short, quick whistles and then a longer flat whistle. Did Shakespeare hear hedgehogs courting one night, and did their sounds inspire him to mention hedgehogs in his plays?

The ancient Egyptians revered hedgehogs and made objects, flasks, and ceramic jewelry in the image of hedgehogs. Some authors say that the ancient Egyptians believed hedgehogs were capable of reincarnation. Hedgehogs hibernate when conditions are cold. Hibernation, and recovery from hibernation, inexplicable to the Egyptians of that time, could have easily been misinterpreted as recovery from death. It would surely have drawn awe and admiration from an ancient civilization that placed great importance on the concept of life after death.

Pliny the Elder (AD 23–79) was a Roman naturalist who wrote 37 tomes about natural history and mistakenly believed hedgehogs could roll onto apples that had fallen to the ground, skewer the fruits on their quills, and transport them on their backs. Other authors claimed hedgehogs could climb trees and shake apples out of the trees. In his encyclopedia *Etymologiae*, Saint Isidore of Seville (560–636) wrote that hedgehogs used their quills to slice bunches of grapes off vines and skewer them.

African Pygmy Hedgehog Names Used in Literature

African hedgehog
West African hedgehog
White-bellied hedgehog
Spiny hedgehog
Four-toed hedgehog
Erinaceus albiventris (Wagner 1842)
Atelerix pruneri (Gregory 1975)
Atelerix pruneri (Corbet 1968)
Atelerix albiventris (Gregory 1975)
Heyghoge (Middle English 1450) *heyg* or *hegge* meaning "hedge" or "hedgerow," and *hoge* or *hogge* meaning "pig"
Furze-pig (Old English for "prickly" or "rough," after the gorse plant, or furze plant, *Ulex europaeus*, a spiny plant belonging to the *Fabaceae* family)

In reality, hedgehogs do not skewer or transport fruits or anything else with their quills. However, dirt, debris, and plant particles easily adhere to their quills, especially after they have been "anting" (see "Understanding Your Hedgehog") or sleeping rolled up in a ball with their quills in contact with the ground.

Hedgehogs are also portrayed unrealistically in most children's stories. Lena Anderson's book *Hedgehog's Secret* (2001) describes the hedgehog as a busybody that cooks and sews in preparation for a new baby—baby hedgehog that is! Beatrix Potter's *The Tale of Mrs. Tiggy-Winkle* (1905) presents the hedgehog as a curious washerwoman. In Lewis Carrol's *Alice's Adventures in Wonderland* (1865), Alice plays croquet with a crazed queen, using a live hedgehog for a croquet ball. In 1991, Sonic the Hedgehog, a teal blue animated superhero, blasted into the world of video games with the ability to run faster than the speed of sound.

Although Sonic the Hedgehog is arguably the most famous fictional hedgehog character that most modern-day children will know, the only thing Sonic has in common with real hedgehogs is the ability to swim and to curl into a ball!

Archilocus (approximately 680–640 BCE) the Greek soldier poet reportedly wrote, "The fox knows many things, but the hedgehog knows one big thing." Over time we have pried away some of the hedgehog's secrets and sifted fact from fiction and controversy from confusion. We have learned "many things" about this cute and covert creature. With continued research, observation, and sharing of *accurate* information, perhaps one day we will discover the "one big thing" that the hedgehog knows!

Author's note: Only information that has been researched, referenced, and accurately documented as scientific fact is presented in this book.

Mysterious Natural History

Evolutionarily, the African pygmy hedgehog is one of the most primitive mammals on our planet. Research—from fossil and dental analyses, to molecular genetic (DNA) tests, to comparative studies of the African pygmy hedgehog brain—supports this hypothesis. Hedgehogs have changed very little since their earliest ancestors first wandered the earth millions of years ago. Indeed, the African pygmy hedgehog's taxonomic order, *Erinaceomorpha*, which includes African pygmy hedgehogs and their closest relatives, comprises the world's most ancient eutherian species. Some scientists credit them with having possibly survived since the time of the dinosaurs, although there is disagreement among paleontologists about how many millions of years ago the hedgehog's ancestors existed. Disputed time frames range from the Cretaceous period (145 to 65 million years ago) to the Cretaceous Paleogene boundary, 65 million years ago. Many scientists think that the *Erinaceomorpha* family evolved during the Paleocene period (about 60 million years ago), in what is now North America. From there the family is believed to have spread to Asia during the Eocene period (about 55 million

Eutherian Mammal

Eutherian mammals are a group of animals that are placental, or that are more closely related to placental animals than to marsupials. All nonplacental eutherian mammals are now extinct.

Placental Mammal

Placental mammals bear live young that are nourished in the mother's uterus through a special organ attached to the uterus, called the placenta. Today, all living eutherian mammals are placental.

years ago), spreading to the European continent and on to Africa during the Miocene period (about 20 million years ago).

Note: A 2007 study of newly discovered fossils placed the evolution of eutherian mammals close to the Cretaceous Paleogene boundary in Laurasia, rather than the Cretaceous period in the Southern Hemisphere, as some earlier studies suggested.

One thing is for certain—of all the mammalian species that share the world with us today, hedgehogs and their relatives are among the oldest residents. For any species to survive so long in our turbulent world is truly remarkable. These fantastic time travelers have changed very little since the first ancient eutherian mammals evolved, and by studying hedgehogs, we are granted a rare glimpse into our planet's primeval past.

Bright Future

Unlike some hedgehog species, the African pygmy hedgehog is not endangered. In 1991, African pygmy hedgehog importation from Africa to the United States was banned because African pygmy hedgehogs can carry foot-and-mouth disease and hedgehog imports from Africa were thought to pose a potential risk to livestock in the United States. Imports after 1991 came from New Zealand stock.

African pygmy hedgehog owners quickly rose to meet the challenges of creating breeding colonies and producing high-quality animals in captivity. They joined together and formed clubs and organizations (see "Information") to produce healthy African pygmy hedgehogs for the U.S. pet market. Today's African pygmy hedgehogs all come from animals bred in captivity and raised

Species
Animals that can breed with one another and produce viable, fertile, normal offspring

Hybrid
A hybrid is not a species. A hybrid is the product of two parents that each belong to a different species. Hybrids are usually infertile (sterile). Rarely, individuals of closely related species may interbreed, usually with artificial assistance.

domestically. Thanks to the efforts of dedicated breeders and fanciers, the African pygmy hedgehog's future looks bright and secure.

Species and Hybrids
Some pet publications report that decades ago some fanciers bred Algerian hedgehogs (*Atelerix algirus*) to African pygmy hedgehogs (*Atlelerix albiventris*) and that some of today's hedgehog pets are the descendants of these hybrid matings. Although the two species are similar, scientists have closely studied their chromosomes and found that they are indeed separate species.

Hedgehog species differ in genetic makeup, characteristics, response to environmental influences, geographical range, physiology, reproduction (such as gestation length or breeding season), certain anatomical features, and biology. DNA analysis is the only way to accurately determine if an animal is a hybrid or a true species. Although hedgehogs have been widely studied, a DNA test for hedgehog species or hybrid identification is not available to pet owners at this time. However, if you are wondering if your pet is a true species or a hybrid, it is most likely a true species.

BEFORE YOU BUY

African pygmy hedgehogs are easy to care for, but they also have special requirements, including frequent handling to keep them tame and well socialized. There is much to learn and consider before adding a hedgehog pet to your life. Responsible hedgehog ownership involves planning, long-term commitment, time, and expense—and a lot of fun!

A Prickly Pet

If you are looking for a cute companion that is entertaining, unusual, small, portable, and fun, then an African pygmy hedgehog just might be the perfect match for you. Hedgehogs, however, are not for everyone. Hedgehogs differ from more common pets in many ways. They have unique behaviors and some special requirements. These extraordinary animals can make wonderful pets, but they need owners who understand and appreciate them and know how to take good care of them. Learn as much as you can about hedgehogs, *before* adding one to your family!

Special Considerations

You and Your Lifestyle

You are the first consideration. How you live, where you live, what you do, and how busy you are—even your sleep schedule—are all important factors in assessing how well a hedgehog will fit into your lifestyle. The addition of a new hedgehog into your life should be a happy, positive experience. It should not be a stressful burden or a disappointment.

People who care for pets gain many psychological and physiological benefits from the human-animal bond they form. Pet owners feel needed and loved because their animals depend on them for food and care and give companionship in return. Medical research suggests that people who own pets may even live longer. Sadly, some people (such as those with allergies or with compromised immune systems) simply cannot have animals in their homes, no matter how much they love them. It is possible to develop allergies to animal saliva, dander, urine, and cage bedding material. If you tend to develop allergies, discuss them with your physician before acquiring any new pet.

States That Currently Restrict Keeping African Pygmy Hedgehogs

Arizona: Strict housing requirements that are difficult to meet, making it almost impossible to keep the animals.

California: Not allowed

Georgia: Breeders may obtain licenses to keep African pygmy hedgehogs for breeding, but the animals that are produced must be shipped outside the state.

Hawaii: Not allowed

New York: *Some* areas prohibit hedgehog pets.

Pennsylvania: Not allowed

Some states, counties, and districts prohibit keeping African pygmy hedgehogs as pets. Laws change periodically, so check with your state and local authorities before you purchase an African pygmy hedgehog. You can obtain updated information from your local animal control agency and your state's fish and wildlife department.

In jurisdictions where African pygmy hedgehogs are prohibited as pets, authorities can confiscate and euthanize them and owners can be fined.

Age and Longevity

An African pygmy hedgehog's life span varies for each animal, depending on the care and nutrition it receives, and its genetics. With excellent care, hedgehogs can live from three to six years, perhaps longer, so hedgehog ownership is a long-term commitment. Throughout the years, you will become extremely attached to your little companion. Sadly, at some time, you will experience the grief that accompanies the eventual, and inevitable, illness or death of

your beloved pet. The most difficult thing about caring for and loving an African pygmy hedgehog is having to part with one.

Your Expectations

If you don't expect your African pygmy hedgehog to be similar to common pets and let him surprise you with his unique behaviors and personality, you won't be disappointed—you'll be delighted! Understanding hedgehogs and their instinctive and natural behaviors will allow you to appreciate them for what they are—wild, primitive animals that are raised domestically and can be tamed. Each animal has its own personality. Some hedgehogs are more social than others. Some enjoy sitting on laps and others prefer to explore and will not remain in one place for long. Hedgehogs can bond with their owners and are friendly with people they trust.

Some hedgehogs can be trained to use a litter box, but when they are exploring, they pay little attention to where they defecate and urinate. They eliminate where and when the need arises, even if they are in someone's lap.

Hedgehogs are creatures of the twilight and dark hours and are active intermittently during the day. During their waking hours, hedgehogs are almost continually on the move. Your pet can be noisy as he snuffles about and forages, explores his surroundings, pushes objects, and runs in his exercise wheel. If you are a light sleeper, place your hedgehog's enclosure away from the bedroom. However, if you are a night owl yourself, a hedgehog can make a very entertaining late-night friend.

The Right Timing

"Impulse buyers" buy pets on the spur of the moment, without first learning about the

species and the care it requires. They often regret their purchase when they realize their expectations for the animal were unreasonable, or that the animal requires more time and care than they thought. Hedgehogs purchased by impulse buyers often end up neglected, unwanted, confined, or abandoned at animal shelters. Others are passed from person to person. Even worse, some irresponsible people release their hedgehogs to the wild, where they cannot survive, and where they die from exposure, starvation, or predators, or are run over by a vehicle.

Hedgehogs should have high-quality care for their entire lives. Fortunately, hedgehog rescue organizations exist, but making wise decisions about hedgehog ownership from the onset will help reduce the need for hedgehog rescues.

If you are already convinced that a hedgehog is the perfect pet for you, make sure the timing is perfect, too. If you have several obligations and your free time is limited, or if you are changing jobs, moving, getting married, returning to school, or going on vacation, postpone your purchase until you have more time to enjoy your new pet.

Hedgehog ownership and care is a responsibility that each person has to assume individually. Don't buy a hedgehog for someone else as a "surprise." Most people want to choose their own pets to make sure they are a good match and have the personalities and characteristics they want.

Cost

African pygmy hedgehog prices vary with supply and demand, the age of the animal, how tame it is, its color, and sometimes its sex (females may be more expensive than males).

The greatest expense of hedgehog ownership is not the purchase price of the animal, but the costs involved in time, housing, bedding, food, space, accessories, and veterinary care.

Time

African pygmy hedgehogs are not demanding pets, but they *do* require adequate time for *daily* care, health observations, and *frequent* gentle handling to keep them tame and social. The size of your pet's enclosure will determine how often he should be cleaned. Fresh water and food must

be provided daily. Take time every day to hold and visit with your little companion. Handling is important to keep your hedgehog tame and friendly and maintain the bond between you both. While you are holding your hedgehog, check him thoroughly to be sure he is healthy. Visiting, handling, feeding, cleaning, and watering take only a few minutes a day—a small investment to ensure that your bright-eyed, spiny companion is healthy and content.

Materials

African pygmy hedgehogs require a few basic essentials: safe, comfortable, escape-proof housing; nutritious food; safe, absorbent bedding material; a water bottle and dishes; hideaways; and an exercise wheel.

African pygmy hedgehogs don't always "play" with toys, but they enjoy interesting things to smell and explore. Favorite hedgehog items include hiding places, objects to safely climb, tubes, tunnels, pots, and gravel baths.

Space

Your hedgehog requires more space than most similarly sized pets. In the wild, hedgehogs can cover a large area during their explorations as they forage for food. Ideally, your hedgehog should have a large, *safe*, enclosed area to roam during the evening. A small, hard plastic children's swimming pool, or plastic concrete mixing tub, works well. If that is not possible, find time to let your hedgehog out while you can directly supervise him. Make sure he doesn't get into trouble!

Other Household Pets

Hedgehogs are solitary animals by choice. They don't need the companionship of other animals, especially not animals of a different species. To be safe, keep your African pygmy hedgehog away from other animals. If you decide to introduce your hedgehog to other pets, do so cautiously to make sure your hedgehog is not harmed or frightened. *To prevent accidental* injury, never leave your pets alone together, no matter how compatible they seem to be.

Hedgehogs have a very keen sense of smell, so they know when there are other animals nearby. Your hedgehog could be frightened by other animals, especially if they come near your hedgehog's enclosure or cage. Mother hedgehogs are very sensitive and should not be disturbed or they may kill, and even cannibalize, their babies.

Hedgehogs are avid explorers and good climbers. To prevent possible escape and accident, make sure the lids and doors to your hedgehog's cage are securely fastened and place the cage well out of reach of the family dog, cat, ferret, reptiles, birds, or other pets.

Selecting a Veterinarian

Hedgehogs are generally hardy animals that do very well with loving care and good nutrition, but if your tiny spiny companion is sick or injured, he will need veterinary care.

The sooner your pet is diagnosed and treated, the better his chances are for recovery. It is also important to know the cause of illness to be sure that the problem is not contagious to you or your other pets.

Some veterinarians specialize in wild and exotic animals, or have a special interest in them. Hedgehogs have nutritional, housing, and care requirements that are different from common companion animals. Although hedgehogs are reported to be resistant to certain toxins, the fact remains that hedgehogs can be very sensitive to certain medications used for treating more common pets.

Select a veterinarian *before* you purchase your hedgehog and *before* he needs health

= TIP =

Essentials of Good Hedgehog Care
- ✔ Nutritious, balanced diet and fresh water
- ✔ Plenty of space to run, play, and forage
- ✔ Clean, dry, draft-free housing
- ✔ Safe, clean bedding material
- ✔ Comfortable temperature and humidity
- ✔ Hideaways and exercise wheel
- ✔ Toys and interesting cage furniture for social enrichment
- ✔ Grooming as necessary
- ✔ Lots of love and attention from you

care. That way, you won't lose precious time during a possible emergency situation.

You and your veterinarian will work together to ensure your little companion's health throughout his life. Be as particular about choosing a veterinarian as you are about selecting your own doctor.

✔ Find a veterinarian who appreciates hedgehogs as much as you do and who has expertise in treating them. Ask hedgehog breeders which veterinarians they recommend. Personal recommendations are among the best ways to find a good veterinarian. The Association of Exotic Mammal Veterinarians and the American Veterinary Medical Association can give you a list of veterinarians in your area (see "Information").

✔ Consider location. Ideally you should be able to drive to the veterinarian's within a reasonable amount of time in case of an emergency.

✔ Ask if the doctor makes house calls. Sometimes transporting small, sick animals can stress them.

Choosing Your African Pygmy Hedgehog

Where to Find Your Hedgehog

Whenever possible, it is best to purchase your African pygmy hedgehog directly from a knowledgeable, reputable breeder. If you purchase from a breeder, you may have the opportunity to see the animals and facilities, ask the breeder questions, and have a greater selection of animals from which to choose. The breeder can also give you information about the animal's age, health, parents, genetic background, health guarantees, and sales contracts. The breeder can recommend a veterinarian experienced in treating hedgehogs.

You can find breeders by contacting hedgehog clubs and associations, searching the Internet, and finding advertisements in pet magazines, such as *Critters USA* (see "Information"). Your veterinarian may also be able to recommend breeders to you.

To ensure their animals' safety and know their animals are placed in loving homes, many breeders require the buyer to fill out an application form and meet with them in person before concluding a sale. Be prepared to drive to pick up your hedgehog in person, as many breeders will not send their animals by air.

Some pet stores sell African pygmy hedgehogs, but stores usually cannot provide as much information about the animal as the breeder can. Take time to handle and examine the hedgehogs to see how tame and healthy they are before you buy one. This can be difficult in a store environment. Pet stores sometimes house males and females together, in which case the hedgehog you buy may be pregnant without your knowing!

Quick Hedgehog Health Check

✔ Normal weight, not too fat (unable to curl into a ball) and not too thin (abdomen should not be concave and animal should not feel bony)

✔ Eyes open, bright, clear, and free of discharge

✔ Ears and nose clean and free of discharge

✔ Skin and quills clean and healthy; no excessive quill loss

✔ Ears and skin free of parasites, sores, crusts, scabs; normal color (not reddened and no yellow tinge)

✔ Anal and genital areas clean; no signs of discharge or diarrhea

✔ Feet clean, free of sores; no overgrown nails

After you have gained experience with hedgehogs, you might want to adopt one from a hedgehog rescue association. These animals may have behavior or health problems or special needs, so an experienced hedgehog owner is a good match for them.

How to Choose Your Hedgehog

You may be tempted to take home the first hedgehog you find, but it is wiser to visit as many breeders and look at as many animals as you can before making a selection. This way you can compare the animals' overall health, temperament (character, personality), and sociability; the cleanliness of their environment; color varieties; health guarantees; sales contracts; and prices.

Your hedgehog's health and temperament are the most important selection criteria. Every animal is different, so take your time to handle and examine each hedgehog you are considering. Start by observing the animals. Then select one that appeals to you, scoop him up in both hands (see "HOW-TO: Handling Your Hedgehog") and wait for him to relax, uncurl, and show interest in you.

When a hedgehog is relaxed, it flattens its quills and the quills point toward the back of the body and feel like stiff brush bristles. When frightened, the hedgehog curls into a prickly ball with quills crisscrossed and projecting in all directions. Handling a hedgehog in this position can be difficult and uncomfortable. The quills can cause a prickling, irritating, or burning sensation in some people. People with delicate skin may find it easier to hold a hedgehog if they wear protective gloves.

Some hedgehogs remain calm while being handled and enjoy the attention. Others are in a hurry to get away and go somewhere. Many hedgehogs need time before they relax, peek out, uncurl, and explore your fingers and hands. If the hedgehog you select is calm and uncurls, you can check him for signs of good health.

Hedgehogs that are easily startled or fearful may curl into a tight ball and remain that way for a long time. In rare instances, a frightened hedgehog may nip. If the animal refuses to uncurl, or if he makes threatening "clicks" at you, then continue your search for a more sociable, friendly individual.

You will quickly learn how tame and social the hedgehog is as you spend time with him and handle him. The friendlier your pet is, the more you will enjoy each other's company.

Twelve Questions to Ask the Breeder

1. How old is the hedgehog?
2. What sex is it?
3. What does it eat and which commercial hedgehog diet does the breeder recommend?
4. What kind of housing is it used to?
5. What kind of personality/temperament does the hedgehog have?
6. What do the health guarantee and sales contract include?
7. Can the breeder provide a copy of the animal's medical record?
8. Is the breeder available to answer future questions?
9. If, for some reason, you can no longer keep your hedgehog, is the breeder willing to take it back or help you place your pet in a new home?
10. Can you visit the breeder's facilities?
11. Can the breeder recommend a veterinarian with hedgehog expertise?
12. Is there a local hedgehog club to join?

Important! Be prepared to answer the many questions the breeder will ask you, too!

Male or Female?

Both male and female hedgehogs make wonderful companions. Both sexes are equally tame and social in their interactions with their owners, as long as they are socialized and handled frequently, gently, and kindly. The main considerations are as follows:

✔ Males are usually larger than females.

✔ Females tend to have more reproductive health problems (including cancer and infections) than male hedgehogs, so they may cost more in veterinary care.

✔ A female hedgehog that was recently housed with a male may already be pregnant.

If you want to raise hedgehogs, you will obviously need at least one pair to begin your project (see "Raising African Pygmy Hedgehogs").

However, it's best for new owners to keep just one hedgehog for a while and learn as much as possible about the species before embarking on such a major undertaking as hedgehog reproduction! Hedgehogs are naturally solitary animals, so your hedgehog doesn't need a friend.

It is easy to tell the difference between a male and female African pygmy hedgehog. The male's penile sheath resembles a small raised belly button on the abdomen. The distance from the urinary tract opening (urethral orifice) to the anus is called the *ano-genital distance*. This distance is short in females.

How Many Hedgehogs to Keep?

The number of hedgehogs you keep depends on how much time, space, and money you have

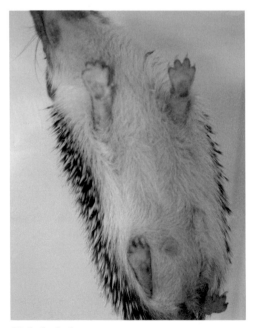

Male hedgehog

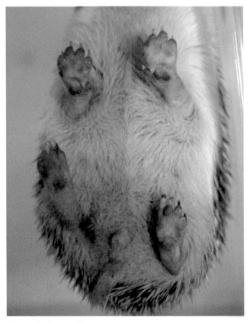

Female hedgehog

Hedgehog Terms of Endearment
Adult hedgehogs: Hedgies, hogs
Male hedgehogs: Boars
Female hedgehogs: Sows
Baby hedgehogs: baby hedgies, hoglets, pups, cubs

to dedicate to them. If you are raising hedgehogs, you will keep two to several animals. If you just want a companion, one is plenty. Keep your hedgehog population reasonable so that most of the time you spend with your hedgehogs is not spent cleaning up after them but having fun with them instead!

✔ *Hedgehogs are naturally solitary animals.*

✔ *It is safest to house hedgehogs individually.*

✔ *Never house male hedgehogs together.* Males will fight and injure each other.

✔ Do not house a male and a female together unless you are breeding them.

✔ Housing female hedgehogs together is not recommended. Some females get along together as long as there is plenty of space and hiding places, and enough food and water for all of them. With group housing there is no control over each animal's food and water consumption. There is usually one greedy glutton that eats most of the food and gains too much weight while the others lose weight.

✔ Fights can break out suddenly among previously compatible females and they can injure each other.

Children and Hedgehogs

Hedgehogs are not ideal pets for very young children. Small children have difficulty holding hedgehogs because of the prickly spines and because children have small hands. A child can

accidentally drop a hedgehog, causing injury, especially if the hedgehog startles the child by puffing or snorting. On rare occasion, a fearful hedgehog might nip a child. It is safer for small children to observe hedgehogs in their enclosures rather than try to hold them.

African pygmy hedgehogs make interesting and educational pets for older, mature children who can learn the proper way to handle a hedgehog (see "HOW-TO: Handling Your Hedgehog").

Children can learn a lot from a hedgehog, including the importance of humane treatment and good care. Children can participate in the animal's daily care. Of course, hedgehog ownership is a long-term commitment and the animal's care will always be *your* responsibility.

Your Favorite Hedgehog

Choose your pet according to its health, personality, physical attributes, and your personal preferences. Of all the hedgehogs you handle and hold, the healthiest and friendliest will probably be the one to weave its way into your heart. The hardest thing about choosing an African pygmy hedgehog is leaving the other hedgehogs behind!

UNDERSTANDING YOUR HEDGEHOG

The African pygmy hedgehog's instincts, senses, behaviors, and communication reflect millions of years of ancestral development that have allowed it to survive to this day. The better you understand your African pygmy hedgehog, the more you will appreciate and enjoy him.

African pygmy hedgehogs are primitive yet complicated creatures. They are driven by instinct, senses, curiosity, and food! Hedgehogs survive, communicate, and find food using their keen senses of smell, hearing, touch, and taste. They have relatively poor eyesight. Hedgehogs express fear, uncertainty, protection, trust, and contentment with their body language and vocalizations. Some hedgehogs are friendly and easy to tame. Others may never be completely tamed.

Hedgehogs are quick to snort, huff, hiss, and roll into a defensive ball when they feel threatened. This behavior is often triggered by a loud noise or sudden disturbance. With gentle handling, patience, and socialization, a hedgehog may be encouraged to relax, uncurl, and meet the person holding it.

Here is some information to help you interpret your hedgehog's behavior, body language, and vocalizations.

The Basics

Hedgehogs depend on their senses for information about their environment and behave accordingly. Their keenest senses are smell (olfaction), hearing (auditory), and touch (tactile). They have relatively poor vision.

Sense of Smell (Olfactory Sense)

Sense of smell is very important for African pygmy hedgehogs to find food, explore their surroundings, and detect and identify other animals, including potential mates and predators.

The parts of the hedgehog's brain related to the sense of smell (the olfactory lobes) are very well developed in African pygmy hedgehogs, as is the "accessory olfactory system" (Jacobson's organ, or vomeronasal organ [VNO]).

When hedgehogs encounter an interesting scent, they sometimes show a Flehmen response, in which the animals raise their heads, lift their lips, and breathe in the new

Wash your hands after handling food and before handling your hedgehog, and don't let your hedgehog lick you, or you may be mistaken for food and be nipped!

Sense of Hearing (Auditory Sense)

African pygmy hedgehogs have very keen hearing. Hedgehogs rely on hearing to forage for live food, such as insects, and to listen for danger.

Baby hedgehogs make high-frequency sounds to communicate with their mothers. Using specialized equipment researchers have confirmed that hedgehogs can make a variety of sounds in the 40 kHz to 90 kHz range (well above the human hearing range of 20 Hz to 20 kHz).

Sense of Sight

Although hedgehogs have well-developed eyes, they appear to have poor vision and poor depth perception. They cannot judge heights and can easily fall from tables and countertops.

Hedgehog retinas have only rod cells, which are useful for night vision. There are no cone cells in the hedgehog's retina. Cone cells

scent toward the VNO. The VNO detects odors, pheromones, and chemical signals and relays them directly to the accessory olfactory bulb, rather than the main olfactory bulb. For this reason, the VNO has been called an "alternate route to the brain" because it bypasses the cerebral cortex. The VNO has also been called a "sixth sense," as it appears to play a very important role in animal communication, identifying social signals, and influencing behaviors such as reproduction, mating, and maternal behavior. Some researchers think that the VNO plays a significant role in stimulating the hedgehog's "anting" behavior (see page 32).

Sense of Taste

Taste and smell are closely related. Hedgehogs sample things by smelling, licking, and tasting them. Hedgehogs may "ant" after smelling or tasting an interesting item.

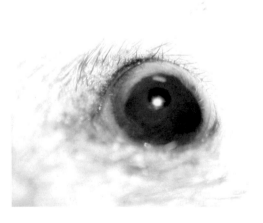

operate in bright light, are responsible for high-acuity vision, and enable complete color vision. Hedgehogs probably see only in shades of black, white, and gray.

Sense of Touch (Tactile Sense)

Studies of the African pygmy hedgehog's brain show that the large facial vibrissae (whiskers) that help the hedgehog navigate in the dark have a small representation in the somatosensory areas of the brain. These complicated areas of the brain process information from numerous sensory receptors and identify sensations such as touch, temperature, and pain. Surprisingly, the African pygmy hedgehog's tiny microvibrissae have a greatly enlarged corresponding area in the cortex of the brain. This means that these tiny hairs just

below the rhinarium (the hairless, moist areas around the nostrils) likely play a very important role in identifying food and probably play a much larger sensory role than the larger, longer facial whiskers do.

Behavior

African pygmy hedgehogs are very expressive. You will easily recognize the times your hedgehog feels comfortable and secure by his body language and the sounds he makes (vocalizations). Hedgehogs are active in the evening and crepuscular (most active at dusk and dawn). They wake periodically throughout the day and are very active when they are awake, spending most of their time foraging for food, exploring, and running in their exercise wheels.

Anting ("Anointing," "Self-Anointing")

When a hedgehog encounters a strange or interesting object or scent, the animal may lick and chew until it produces a large quantity of foamy, frothy saliva. The hedgehog then spreads the saliva over its quills with its long tongue. This behavior is called *anting*. Hedgehogs are flexible and can bend to coat their sides, flanks, and backs with saliva. Sometimes they fall over in the process.

Anting starts at about three weeks of age. Baby hedgehogs will ant after licking their mothers' quills. Some hedgehogs ant frequently, whereas others seldom engage in this curious activity.

Theories about why hedgehogs ant:

✔ To smell like new objects they have encountered, or to smell like the surrounding environ-ment, or to hide their natural scent from predators
✔ To dissipate heat (cool down)
✔ For parasite control
✔ To coat themselves with toxins for protection

Some reports say that hedgehogs are more resistant to certain toxins than other animals. One scientist reported that hedgehogs may lick the toxins off of toads and then spread them on their quills with their saliva, to make their quills offensive to predators and to be more dangerous to touch.

Anting is not new in nature. *Anting* is a behavior documented in some bird species. The birds rub ants (and other insects) on their feathers, presumably to make the insects dis-charge their toxins (formic acids) and create a layer of offensive chemicals on the feathers, thereby providing the bird more protection from predators and perhaps helping to reduce the number of external parasites.

People can suffer from contact dermatitis and allergic reactions from being poked by hedgehog quills. A study of hedgehog saliva would be worthwhile to identify possible sub-stances that can cause allergic reactions in some individuals and bacteria that contribute to skin irritation.

Quill Raising

A relaxed hedgehog lays its quills relatively flat on its body, pointing backward. When frightened or disturbed, the animal erects its quills. Quills are raised individually by special-ized erector muscles to which they are attached. Some quill areas can be raised inde-pendently of others. For example, the quills on the brow can be raised and pulled forward

where they split into five branches, controlling the spines on the forehead. The *panniculus carnosus* is a thin, subcutaneous striated muscle under the fatty tissue that envelops the body. The *orbicularis panniculi* muscle encircles the hedgehog's body under the edge of the spiny dorsum, pulling the skin and quills around the body as the hedgehog tucks its head, limbs, and belly inward. The result is a tight, protective ball with crisscrossed quills. It is very difficult to force a hedgehog to uncurl.

Hedgehogs curl into a ball as a means of protection and also to conserve body heat.

Aggressive and Protective Behaviors

Lunging and head butting are forms of protective and aggressive behaviors. The hedgehog pulls the quills on its crown forward and then lunges, using its quills as weapons. Males headbutt and bite when they fight. Mother hedgehogs lunge, head-butt, and bite anything they perceive as a threat to their babies or as an intruder in their territory—including your hands.

independently from the quills on the back, whether the animal curls into a ball or not.

Curling into a Ball

Hedgehogs have well-developed, specialized muscles that enable them to curl into a tight ball. Dorsal (back) muscles attach from near the tail base and continue to the base of the skull,

Biting

Hedgehogs rarely bite. Biting can follow licking and nipping if the animal thinks an object (or finger!) is edible. Hedgehogs also bite or nibble on each other's ears. Hedgehogs can injure their mouths from biting on each other's quills. Males can seriously injure each other when they fight. Mother hedgehogs with babies can bite and cannibalize their young if they are disturbed.

Elimination

Hedgehogs tend to defecate and urinate in one area of their cage, usually in a corner. When they run loose in a large enclosure, they often eliminate near the wall of the enclosure, rather than in the center.

Hibernation

Hedgehogs hibernate in adverse cold conditions to conserve energy. During hibernation the animal's breathing, heart rate, and metabolism slow significantly. Hedgehogs that are well nourished and housed in comfortable temperatures (75°–85°F [24°–29°C] will not hibernate.

It is dangerous for a pet African pygmy hedgehog's health to hibernate. The stresses caused by hibernation make the animal more susceptible to disease and infection. To prevent hibernation, African pygmy hedgehogs should be housed at temperatures between 75° and 85°F (24°–29°C). At temperatures below 60°F (17°C) to 47°F (8°C) hedgehogs will enter torpor (a state of inactivity, with a drop in metabolism and body temperature) and hibernate.

Heat Stress

At temperatures above 85°F (29°C), your hedgehog can suffer from heat stress.

When hedgehogs are overheated, they pant and stretch out flat on their bellies to cool down. (See the chapter titled "Health" to learn how to treat this emergency situation.) Hedgehogs suffering from heatstroke die quickly.

Social Life

Hedgehogs are solitary animals. Males are not compatible and will fight. Males and females find each other only for mating and then go their separate ways, leaving the mother to raise the babies without any help from the father. When the babies are weaned, they too go their separate ways.

Body Language

Curiosity and Interest

When hedgehogs are interested in something, foraging, or exploring, they may sniff and snuffle loudly and walk with a rolling, waddle-like gait. The body will be relaxed, with quills flattened, head extended, and nose to the ground, or in the air, searching out scents.

Fear

If hedgehogs are startled or frightened, they pull their quills over their brows to protect the face, raise their quills, or curl into a ball. Hedgehogs may huff, puff, hiss, snort, click, pop, and make other sounds to deter predators.

Vocalizations

Using sophisticated equipment, scientists have studied a wide variety of sounds hedgehogs make.

Hedgehog Vocalizations

Sounds	Meaning	Males	Females	Babies
		Males	Females	Babies
Clicking, popping	Protective or aggressive action intended to threaten, frighten, or intimidate a perceived threat. Hedgehog may bite.	x	x	
Clucking	Males may cluck during courtship; females cluck when retrieving babies to the nest.	x	x	
Hiss, snort, huff, puff	Hedgehog feels threatened and is trying to intimidate intruders. Hedgehogs hiss and snort when they head-butt.	x	x	
Purr-like vibration	Content, calm. This sound is similar to the vibration sound made by an apprehensive hedgehog, so assess the situation to know if the sound indicates contentment or fear.	x	x	
Peep (soft)	Contentment, or baby's call to mother; baby is hungry.		x	x
Scream	Aggression, agitation, pain, usually male-to-male encounters	x	x	
Serenade, singing	Repeated squeaks, similar to a bird call, made during courtship	x		
Sniffing, snuffling	Content, calm, relaxed, exploring	x	x	
Twitter	Soft sound; mouth is usually closed while emitting the sound. A twitter can last from 60 to 90 seconds. Young animals less than 3 months of age, especially newborns, twitter.	x	x	x
Vibration, continual	Fear, anxiety, apprehension; often precedes popping or clicking	x	x	
Whine	Male searching for mate	x		
Whistle	Distress call; neonates' call to mother			x

ACCOMMODATIONS FOR YOUR HEDGEHOG

African pygmy hedgehogs are not demanding pets. There are many things you can do to make sure your hedgehog has everything he needs to be healthy, content, and safe in your home.

African pygmy hedgehogs require a few basic housing essentials. Fortunately, these are easy and inexpensive to provide.

You can design a housing setup for your hedgehog that is creative and convenient for you, and as complex or simple as you please. Your pet can adapt to a wide variety of housing options available, as long as there is *plenty of space to explore*, there are *lots of places to hide and sleep*, and the *housing is safe, clean, and escape-proof.*

Special Housing Considerations

1. *African pygmy hedgehogs should be housed individually.* They are solitary animals that do not normally enjoy interacting, socializing, or living with other animals. Fights among females can break out unexpectedly, even among females that seemed previously compatible. Males fight, even if they are siblings. They head-butt, hiss, growl, and bite and can injure each other.

2. *Keep males and females separated to prevent unwanted pregnancies.* If you are raising hedgehogs, you may temporarily house a male and female together, but supervise them carefully for compatibility.

3. *African pygmy hedgehogs need a lot of space to explore.* Hedgehogs are very active and inquisitive animals. They need a safe, "hedgehog-proof" space to exercise to keep them healthy and prevent obesity. *Do not allow your hedgehog to run loose in the home unsupervised.*

4. *African pygmy hedgehogs are good climbers and excellent escape artists.* The walls of your pet's enclosure must be smooth and

high to prevent escape. Recommended minimum height is 12 inches (30 cm) or more, depending on the size of the hedgehog. Make sure all cage doors and latches are closed and fastened securely.

5. *Wire cage floors, exercise wheels with wire floors, and wire-wall enclosures are not suitable for hedgehogs.* Hedgehogs have delicate, sensitive feet, and wire floors cause foot sores. Hedgehogs can catch or trap their feet and legs in between wire bars or in the wire mesh and injure or break their limbs. Wire may contain lead, zinc, paint, plastic coatings, or other kinds of substances that are toxic for your pet. Cages and exercise wheels should always have safe, solid flooring to prevent injury. The floor of your pet's cage should be made of a solid, smooth, hard plastic or safe metal, such as stainless steel. Wire bars should run in a vertical direction, so that the hedgehog cannot climb or injure his legs and feet.

Housing Options

The cage, style, materials, and size you choose for your hedgehog's housing will depend on the amount of space available in your home—and your imagination. You don't necessarily have to buy a cage from the pet store. In fact, most cages available in pet stores are not specifically designed for hedgehogs. The important thing is for the cage to fit your pet's needs. There are lots of inexpensive housing options that are safe, easy to clean, spacious, and will work very well for your hedgehog.

Housing options:

✔ Small, hard plastic children's wading pool available at most toy stores or plastic concrete mixing tub from the hardware store

✔ Very large plastic storage box available at most office supply stores, minimum of 2 feet × 2 feet (60 cm × 60 cm), larger size is preferable. Do not use plastic lid, as it will not allow enough ventilation!

Housing Options

Housing/Cage Style	Advantage	Disadvantage	Make Sure
Children's plastic wading pool; plastic concrete mixing tub	Provides environmental enrichment with large area to play and explore; easy to observe pet; room for toys and hideaways; easy to clean; inexpensive; well-ventilated	Takes up large amount of floor space	Keep away from other animals
Large plastic boxes	Easy to see pet; easy to clean; inexpensive	Must be large to allow adequate ventilation; humidity and ammonia can build up	Keep away from other animals
Aquarium	Easy to see pet; protects from drafts; muffles loud sounds; nonporous; no litter scatter	Poor ventilation; humidity and ammonia can build up; heavy to move; water bottle attachments take up inside space	A snug-fitting, snap-on or clip-on mesh lid is necessary to prevent escape.
Wire cages	Easy to see pet; well ventilated; easy to clean; door at top or side for convenience	Hedgehogs can climb and escape or be injured; wire bars and mesh cause foot sores; wire may contain toxic metals and coatings	Vertical bars are preferable to prevent climbing, injury, and escape.
Wooden cages	Easy to build to any specifications; inexpensive	Porous and difficult to disinfect or sanitize unless a safe, protective coating is applied or the floor is lined with vinyl or plastic.	Do not use cedar or chemically treated or toxic woods. Do not coat with toxic paints or toxic varnishes.
Dog travel kennel	Easy to clean; comes in various sizes	Can be dark inside	Fasten door latch securely. Make sure there is enough ventilation

Note: All enclosures should be in a safe location away from other animals and small children.

✔ Large selection of wire cages available in pet stores, such as those designed for guinea pigs

✔ Wooden cages

✔ Well-ventilated dog travel kennel, minimum 23 inches × 32 inches (58 cm × 80 cm) and 27 inches (68 cm) high. Kennels smaller than this size are too dark inside and have poor air circulation.

✔ Plexiglas aquarium (minimum 30-gallon [115-L] size or larger to allow for sufficient air circulation)

You can make your pet's environment more interesting by connecting housing units together with PVC pipe so that your hedgehog can tunnel from one den to another.

Housing Requirements

1. Minimum cage size for one African pygmy hedgehog

Four square feet (1.5 m) minimum cage floor space

2 feet × 2 feet (60 cm × 60 cm)

The more space you can give your hedgehog, the better!

2. Cage walls should be smooth and high to prevent escape (at least 12 inches [30 cm] high).

3. Cages and cage floors and floor pans should be safe, easy to clean, nonporous, hard plastic or metal, such as stainless steel. The materials should be resistant to moisture, salts, and cleansers.

4. Cage floor pans should be at least 6 inches (15 cm) deep to prevent loose bedding from falling out of the cage. Keep at least 2 inches (5 cm) of bedding in the cage pan to provide a soft surface for your pet's feet and adequate absorption. The cage pan can be lined with newspaper, and bedding can be placed on top of the newspaper.

Housing Conditions

Temperature

African pygmy hedgehogs are sensitive to temperature extremes and high humidity. They should be comfortably housed between 75°F (24°C) and 85°F (29°C).

✔ Do not place your pet's home enclosure near heaters, fireplaces, furnaces, fans, or in areas of direct sunlight.

✔ Do not place your hedgehog's home in drafty areas where your pet could become chilled and develop respiratory infections and pneumonia.

✔ Do not let your hedgehog hibernate! Hibernating is stressful and dangerous for your pet.

Ventilation

Adequate ventilation in your hedgehog's home enclosure is very important. Housing should be well ventilated but not drafty.

Humidity

Humidity should range from 40 percent to 55 percent. If your hedgehog is suffering from respiratory problems, increasing humidity to 55 percent can make breathing easier. You can buy an inexpensive hygrometer from your local hardware store to measure humidity.

Lighting (Photoperiod)

The number of hours of light exposure an animal receives daily is called the *photoperiod*.

African pygmy hedgehogs are active during the night with peaks of activity during twilight and dawn. This crepuscular activity schedule can change depending on outside influences, such as lighting. Hedgehogs also adapt to their owners' schedules and will be active during parts of the day.

Place your hedgehog's enclosure in an area of your home that is lighted during the day and dark at night. An ideal lighting system is 12 hours of light during the day and 12 hours of dark at night.

For reverse lighting, keep your pet's area well lighted during the evening hours and then dark during the normal daylight hours. Or, you can purchase special red light sources from the pet store to use for reverse lighting schedules, just like the ones used in zoological gardens. The red light source is different from regular light and does not disrupt the hedgehog's sleep and reproductive patterns but provides enough light to observe the animal while he is active in the dark.

Sound

African pygmy hedgehogs have excellent hearing and can hear in high-frequency ranges. They are very sensitive to sound and are startled by loud noises. Put your hedgehog's home in a quiet place. Avoid areas of noisy activity or loud sounds, such as doorbells, chiming clocks, barking dogs, televisions, sound systems, vacuum cleaners, and appliances.

Bedding Material

There are many types of bedding material available. Pelleted paper bedding works well for most hedgehogs. Highly absorbent, shredded paper also works well for bedding and environmental enrichment, as hedgehogs enjoy tunneling and hiding under shredded paper.

Some hedgehogs eat their bedding. This can cause intestinal obstruction or choking, so observe your hedgehog closely. If your pet tries to eat his bedding, select a different type of bedding that he doesn't like to eat.

Bedding Materials

Type of Bedding	Advantages
Pelleted paper	Low dust, lower incidence of allergies for people and pets than some other bedding materials; helps prevent skin problems (dermatitis); highly absorbent.
Shredded paper	Provides environmental enrichment because hedgehogs enjoy burrowing and hiding under shredded paper; inexpensive
Newspapers	Inexpensive; readily available
Aspen shavings	Inexpensive
Vellux blanket pieces cut to fit floor space	Washable; sturdy; soft; keeps down dust and allergens
Recycled newspaper pellets and puffs	Cheap; readily available
Pine shavings	Inexpensive
Cedar shavings	None
Corn-cob bedding	None
Terry cloth towels	None

Disadvantages	Recommended?
May cause obstruction if eaten. Slightly more expensive than some bedding materials.	Yes
Less absorbent than pelleted paper	Yes
In the U.S. only nontoxic inks are approved for newspapers; however, other countries' newspapers might contain toxic inks, so check first before using.	Yes
More expensive than pine shavings	Yes
More expensive than shavings and less absorbent; needs frequent washing	Yes
Can cause choking and intestinal obstruction if eaten; can discolor quills; smells when wet.	No
Messy, dusty; humans and animals can develop allergies to the aromatic oils in shavings.	No. There is concern about long-term safety of pine shavings for hedgehog bedding. If you use pine shavings, it is safest to buy cured shavings that have been processed to help remove aromatic oils.
Contain aromatic oils that can be toxic and cause liver damage in some species	No
Can cause allergies and dermatitis; can dry skin and dehydrate newborns, and can stick to ano-genital orifices (anus, urethra, penis sheath), causing obstruction. Hedgehogs may eat corn-cob bedding and can choke on it.	No
Frays easily; when ingested can cause choking or gastrointestinal obstruction; quills and nails may get caught in fabric. Loose threads can wrap around hedgehog feet and limbs and cut off circulation (especially baby hedgehogs).	No

The exercise wheel should be large enough to accommodate your hedgehog comfortably. Wheel diameter should be 10 to 15 inches (25–38 cm) or more, depending on the size of your pet. The wheel should have a solid floor to prevent foot injury and be easy to clean, as hedgehogs often defecate and urinate while running in their wheels.

The Flying Saucer wheel is shaped like a flying saucer and tilted at an angle. It also works well for hedgehogs and is easy to clean.

Some hedgehogs develop obsessive wheel-running behavior, spending most of their waking moments in their exercise wheels until they are exhausted. This can lead to health problems and weight loss. If your hedgehog spends all of his time in the exercise wheel, remove the wheel from your pet's enclosure and put it back in his enclosure when you want your hedgehog to exercise. After your hedgehog has had a nice run, remove the wheel so he can rest.

Never use clumping litter of any kind for bedding. This type of bedding can clump, adhere, or cake on damp areas of the hedgehog's body, such as the urogenital openings (urethra or anus) and cause obstruction, preventing urination and defecation. If eaten, clumping bedding can cause intestinal obstruction and death.

Hedgehog skin is sensitive. Contact with moist, contaminated, and soiled bedding can cause skin problems, such as dermatitis and infections. Be sure to clean your hedgehog's enclosure frequently to prevent health problems—at least once weekly, more often if needed. During the week you can spot-clean soiled areas daily.

Exercise Ball

The use of exercise balls is controversial. Many hedgehogs appear to enjoy exercise balls as a way to briefly explore their surroundings. However, some hedgehogs do not like being confined in an exercise ball.

If you decide to offer your pet an exercise ball, purchase a large size designed for ferrets (volleyball size or larger).

✔ Watch your pet closely to be sure he is not frightened or unhappy in the ball.

✔ If your hedgehog is stressed, remove him from the exercise ball immediately.

✔ Exercise balls should be used for brief time periods only (not more than ten minutes). Hedgehogs become bored when confined in a

Exercise Wheel

An exercise wheel is important for your pet to exercise, maintain body condition, help prevent obesity, and for social enrichment.

small area. Also, humidity and temperature can rise inside an exercise ball after a short time.

Never leave your hedgehog unsupervised in an exercise ball. Your hedgehog may become stressed and need to be removed from the ball. Also, the ball may accidentally come apart and your hedgehog could escape.

Hideaways and Nest Boxes

Your hedgehog needs a variety of places to hide and sleep to feel safe and secure. This is especially important if you are housing a mother and babies.

You can make or purchase hideaways out of many common items, such as ceramic flower-pots, PVC tubes, wooden nest boxes, plastic boxes and "igloos," and artificial logs. You can also make a hiding bag out of soft cotton material or Vellux.

Hideaways are extremely important for your pet's well-being, environmental enrichment, and sleep. Hedgehogs that do not have enough hiding places can become so stressed that they will refuse to eat. Mother hedgehogs need several different hideaways to periodically relocate their babies and sometimes to get away from their babies and rest. Ideally, your pet should have at least three hideaways. The more, the better!

Toys

Toys are a great source of environmental enrichment. Hedgehogs enjoy things that can be explored (hideaways, tunnels, tubes), or butted and pushed around (such as ping-pong balls or small plastic balls suspended from the top of the cage). Some hedgehogs enjoy things they can carry in their mouths, such as soft, tiny stuffed toys.

You can buy cardboard and plastic tunnel tubes from the pet store or make them from PVC pipe material. PVC is safe for your pet, inexpensive, comes in different sizes, can be reused, and is easy to clean.

Every hedgehog is different and not all hedgehogs appreciate toys or play with them. Don't be disappointed if your hedgehog ignores his toys!

Note: Most cardboard tubing (98 to 99 percent) from paper towel rolls, toilet paper rolls,

or gift-wrapping paper rolls are made from recycled materials and may contain ink residues, toxic glues, or other contaminants.

Dust, Water, and Gravel "Baths"

"Baths" are another form of environmental enrichment. Some African pygmy hedgehogs enjoy dust baths. However, dust can irritate a hedgehog's eyes and nose, be messy in the home, and damage electronic equipment. If you offer your pet a dust bath, purchase only a clean dust specifically sold for pet use, such as chinchilla dust. Remove the dust bath after your hedgehog has finished rolling in it, or your hedgehog may also use the dust bath as a litter box!

Some people offer their hedgehogs a shallow dish of water for a play bath. If you choose to do this, make sure your pet truly enjoys playing in water and that this is not stressful for him. Make sure the water is warm, no deeper than 1 inch (2.5 cm), and supervise your pet closely while he plays. Do not leave him alone for a moment. When your hedgehog is finished, dry him thoroughly to make sure he doesn't get chilled.

A gravel bath is a better option than a dust bath or water bath. Many hedgehogs enjoy rolling in a plate of smooth (no sharp edges!), clean, pea gravel (⅛ inch to ¼ inch in diameter [3–5 m]), such as Dorset prewashed Pea Gravel. Gravel baths are dust-free and your pet won't be wet and chilled.

Bottles and Dishes

Your hedgehog should have fresh water available at all times. Although hedgehogs prefer to drink out of a dish, a water bottle has several advantages over a dish. A bottle can hold more water than a dish and can be fastened to the outside of the cage, leaving more cage space available for play. Hedgehogs often soil in their dishes. A bottle keeps water clean and fresh. Most hedgehogs learn to use the bottle's sipper tube immediately.

The disadvantage of using a water bottle is that the sipper tube can get plugged and your pet cannot obtain water. Or, the sipper tube can leak and dampen the bedding and also give the impression that your hedgehog is drinking more water than he really is.

Use only metal sipper tubes (stainless steel is ideal). Do not use plastic sipper tubes. They crack, break, and are difficult to disinfect. Some hedgehogs can chip plastic tubes with their teeth.

Check the bottle and sipper tube twice daily to be sure there is plenty of water and the sipper tube is functioning properly and not plugged or leaking. Clean the bottle and sipper tube thoroughly daily.

Hedgehogs readily eat out of a dish. A broad-based or weighted ceramic crock or stainless steel dish, about 3 to 4 inches (8–10 cm) in diameter and 2 inches (5 cm) deep is difficult to tip and easy to clean.

Litter Box

Some hedgehogs learn to use a litter box. Here's how to train your hedgehog:

1. Choose a litter box large enough to accommodate your hedgehog and easy to clean, such as plastic. Make sure one side of the box is low so that your pet can enter it easily.

2. Hedgehogs tend to choose a specific area or corner in their enclosure to eliminate, so place the litter pan in this area. For hedgehogs that eliminate in corners, a corner litter pan with a low front for easy entry is ideal.

3. Cover the litter box floor with pelleted paper litter. Do not use scented litter, clay, or clumping litter. These materials are not safe for hedgehogs.

4. Collect some of your pet's feces or soiled bedding and place it in the litter box to show your hedgehog where he should go.

5. Be patient. Not all hedgehogs learn to use a litter box. Your hedgehog may take a while to learn, or use the box occasionally, or never use it.

Travel Kennel

You will need to transport your hedgehog when you bring him home, and later when you take him to your veterinarian, to hedgehog shows, or with you on vacation (see "Travel with Your Hedgehog"). Pet stores sell many styles of small dog/cat travel kennels made of durable, easy-to-clean, smooth plastic. These kennels are safe, lightweight, and well ventilated, and have doors that latch securely.

YOUR HEDGEHOG COMES HOME

At last—you've found the perfect hedgehog and it's time to bring him home! There are still a few things left to do to make sure your pet's trip home is pleasant and that he will be safe and content in his new surroundings!

Safety First: Hedgehog Hazards

Before you bring your pet home, check for possible hazards an inquisitive hedgehog could encounter if he were to accidentally escape. Your home can be a dangerous place for a hedgehog on the loose. Let's take a look at some of the many accidents waiting to happen in your home so you can prevent them *before* they occur!

Sticky Traps, Snap Traps, Rodent and Insect Poisons, and Baits

Remove all traps, baits, and poisons that are in your house or garage. They are as deadly for your hedgehog as they are for vermin.

Household Chemicals

Hedgehogs can climb into and hide in cabinets where there are household products such as cleaning agents, bug sprays, paints, fertiliz-ers, and other poisonous chemicals. These substances are extremely dangerous and potentially deadly for your pet if he comes in contact with them.

Appliances

Before you do the laundry, check any piles of clothing lying on the floor and double-check the pockets. Sadly, small pets have been found, too late, inside washers and dryers.

Other Pets

Keep your hedgehog separated from other pets. They can frighten and harm him.

Outside Doors

Make sure all doors to the outside or the garage are closed. If your hedgehog escapes to the garage, he will be exposed to hazards and poisons, such as antifreeze (ethylene

glycol) on the garage floor. Antifreeze has a sweet taste, but is a deadly poison that causes rapid kidney failure.

If your hedgehog escapes outside, he will be almost impossible to find and he will certainly not survive the dangers of automobiles, neighborhood animals, and harsh weather conditions.

Poisonous Plants and Insects

While your little friend is on the loose, he will forage and might sample some greenery. Unfortunately, many household and garden plants are poisonous, so be sure to remove any poisonous plants and fertilizers that could make your runaway sick. Your hedgehog might also eat insects that have been poisoned (for example, snails and slugs that have been exposed to snail bait). Remove all pesticides from the area until you locate your hedgehog.

Note: Cocoa mulch used in gardens is toxic for many animals. It contains a methylxanthine substance similar to caffeine.

Crushing Injuries

If your hedgehog has escaped, be very careful where you step and sit down. Check underneath furniture and pillows, especially under rocking and gliding chairs and lounge chairs where your hedgehog could be caught in the mechanism and crushed.

Purchase Housing, Food, Travel Kennel, and Supplies in Advance

Make sure you have everything you need ready and set up for your new pet *before* you bring him home. Purchase the accommodations and food he will need. Take home some of the same food the breeder or pet store has been feeding your pet, to prevent stress and gastric upset from a sudden change in diet. If you change your hedgehog's diet later on, do so gradually.

Set up your hedgehog's enclosure and accommodations in advance so that when you get home, you can transfer the animal directly into his new environment and he won't have to wait, confused and uneasy, in the travel kennel while you get everything ready.

The Trip Home

Take your hedgehog straight home from the breeder's or pet store. Prepare the travel kennel and give your hedgehog some time to get used to it (see "Travel with Your Hedgehog").

If you need to stop and leave your car for any reason, take your hedgehog with you. *Do not leave your hedgehog in a car on a warm day, even for a few minutes.* The temperature inside the car can quickly soar to above 120°F (49°C) within a few minutes, even with the windows cracked open and the car parked in the shade. Your hedgehog could quickly overheat and die.

Quiet, Please!

When you bring your hedgehog home, place him in his enclosure in a quiet area where he can comfortably hide, sleep, and recover from the stresses of being transported and changing environments. Wait until he feels ready to explore and socialize before you handle him. All of the excitement, new sounds and smells, and changes can be frightening for your tiny new friend. Your hedgehog needs time to adapt to his new home and to get to know you.

Capturing Your Escaped Hedgehog

Hedgehogs are fast runners, good climbers, explorers, and *escape artists*! Even with your best attention to detail, you may find that your pet has somehow escaped from his enclosure.

Here are some tips on where to find your hedgehog and how to capture him.

1. You are more likely to find your hedgehog in the evening hours, as he may be sleeping during the day. Hedgehogs like to hide in dark places. Look for your pet inside closets, cabinets, boxes, containers, laundry baskets, and shoes.

2. Listen for the sounds of your hedgehog snuffling and shuffling about in the evening and follow the sounds. Approach your hedgehog slowly, and gently scoop him up in your hands, or use a small pillowcase or T-shirt to wrap over him.

3. Set your pet's favorite hideaway, cage, or travel kennel on the floor in a quiet area. Leave the door open, bait the inside with a favorite treat, and turn down the lights. Your hedgehog will use his keen sense of smell to find his way to the food bait.

4. Purchase a small humane trap at the local pet shop or feed store, or rent or borrow one from your local animal shelter or veterinarian. If you rent a used trap, disinfect it thoroughly before use. It may have been used to trap sick or wild animals and could have germs on it that are dangerous to your hedgehog.

The best time to hold your hedgehog is when he is awake and in a friendly mood. If your pet is asleep and you wake him up, he might be irritable and not want to be handled or held.

Your hedgehog will learn to recognize your scent if you pick him up with your bare hands. If you prefer to wear gloves and are not allergic to latex, you will find that latex gloves are nonslippery and allow you to feel your pet, and that quills usually do not penetrate them.

Gloves made of leather, heavy fabric, rubber, or vinyl can be cumbersome and make handling difficult. Also, hedgehogs are sometimes stimulated to *ant* when they come in contact with leather.

Two-Handed Method

Approach your hedgehog quietly and calmly from behind. Place your hands to the sides of your pet. Gently glide your hands underneath your hedgehog's body, forming a scoop. As you lift your hedgehog, he might curl into a ball. Give your pet some time and let him sit in the palms of your hands. He should quickly relax, and as he does, he will uncurl and support his feet in your hands. Within a few moments your pet will be peering between your fingers, eager to explore. Very small hedgehogs can be supported with one hand and covered with the other hand.

Keep your pet close to you in case he startles you, so you won't drop him!

Towel Method

Use a soft cotton towel or cloth. Do not use terry cloth or other types of cloth with string loops or holes in it, because toenails and quills can snag in the loose threads and holes. Place the towel on top of your hands before you scoop up your pet, so that the cloth is between your hedgehog and your hands, protecting your hands. When your hedgehog relaxes and uncurls, place the towel on your lap and hold your pet in your lap.

Tabletop Method

Place your hedgehog on a flat surface, such as a tabletop. He will eventually relax and start to explore. If you quickly and gently scoop him up as he starts to walk about, he will be less likely to curl up. Remember that hedgehogs cannot judge heights and easily fall from tabletops. Do not leave your pet unsupervised on the tabletop!

Fearful Hedgehogs

Fearful hedgehogs need more time to relax and uncurl. Find a quiet place to hold your pet. Place a soft cloth on your lap to protect your clothing in case your hedgehog eliminates. Place your hedgehog on top of the cloth. Talk to your pet in a calm, soothing voice. Try stroking him gently, backward, from rump to head to help him relax. If this fails, try gently stroking your pet in a circular motion. This method usually works. Some hedgehogs will be soothed and uncurl when stroked, but others dislike this treatment.

Encourage your hedgehog to be social by offering him a small treat. Hedgehogs are easily distracted and reassured by a tasty morsel. An appetizing mealworm might keep your pet glued to your lap—and cement your friendship!

Handle with special care!

Baby Hedgehogs

Cup both hands together and gently scoop the baby into the palms of your hands. Close your hands and hold the baby gently, but firmly, so he doesn't fall. Don't squeeze him!

Pregnant Hedgehogs

Pregnant hedgehogs must be handled very carefully, especially when they are lifted. Support your pet's body so she is not frightened and doesn't struggle. Don't press on her abdomen or chest. Be gentle!

Warning!
✔ Never scruff your hedgehog, or pick him up by rolling the nape of the neck. This method is dangerous because hedgehogs have very shallow eye orbits, and pulling on the skin around the head and shoulders could cause the eyes to protrude out of their sockets.
✔ Never use forceps or other instruments to grasp your hedgehog.
✔ Do not place your hedgehog in a small amount of water to make him uncurl. Hedgehogs

can become frightened if placed in water while in a curled position and can inhale water into their nostrils and lungs. This cruel method is especially hard on sick or weak hedgehogs.

Ouch!

Hedgehogs rarely bite, although they sometimes nip while sampling their surroundings. If your hedgehog bites and latches on, you can usually make him release his hold by gently placing your finger under his chin.

Warning! Some people suggest spraying a few drops of isopropyl alcohol, lemon juice, or other irritating substances in your hedgehog's mouth to make him release his grip if he bites. This method is dangerous and cruel. You may accidentally get the irritating liquids in your hedgehog's eyes and injure them, or irritate the delicate tissues of your pet's mouth. These substances can cause severe pain in pets with dental problems and mouth sores, or if they come in contact with the eyes. This inhumane method is *not* recommended.

Remember! Wash your hands well after handling your hedgehog, to prevent possible irritation from saliva and the spread of germs!

FEEDING YOUR HEDGEHOG

African pygmy hedgehogs are eager eaters! Although some are particular about their food preferences, most are easy to please. By feeding a variety of nutritious foods, in the right amounts, you can keep your hedgehog healthy and prevent obesity.

Hedgehog Digestive System

The hedgehog's teeth are blunt. The stomach and colon are simple compared with many species, and there is no caecum (a pouch that connects the small intestine with the ascending colon and contains bacteria that help digest cellulose from plant materials).

Hedgehogs digest their food quickly. It takes only 12 to 16 hours for food to travel through a hedgehog's intestines.

Feeding Habits

African pygmy hedgehogs are foragers and spend most of their waking hours searching for food. Hedgehogs find their food primarily through their keen sense of smell and sense of touch. Hedgehogs also use their keen hearing to locate live foods, such as insects, lizards, and newborn ("pinky") mice.

Hedgehogs prefer to drink from dishes, but it is easier to keep water clean and fresh and measure how much your pet drinks if he uses a water bottle. Most hedgehogs quickly learn to use a sipper tube. Heavy ceramic crocks or weighted stainless steel dishes are ideal for hedgehog food bowls. They are difficult to tip over and easy to clean.

Don't be discouraged if your hedgehog spills his food, or urinates or defecates in his dish, or plays with the sipper tube and gets the bedding wet. Simply clean up the mess. Pet hedgehogs are raised domestically, but they are *not* domestic animals. Hedgehogs are wild animals, and "table manners" are not part of natural hedgehog behavior!

What to Feed

One of the most controversial topics in hedgehog health care is the subject of a balanced diet. Although we do not yet know the *exact* dietary needs of African pygmy hedgehogs, recent research has provided valuable information about their food requirements to help us better balance our pets' menus.

Wild hedgehogs live a very different life from those kept in captivity as pets. Their diet varies according to food availability throughout the seasons. We cannot exactly duplicate a hedgehog's "natural diet in the wild," but we can purchase baby mice, bugs, mealworms, small lizards, and other hedgehog delicacies from pet stores to supplement their diet.

Fortunately, African pygmy hedgehogs eat a wide variety of foods, so we have some good options to offer our prickly pets. We know, based on experience, which food combinations work well for most hedgehogs and which foods to avoid.

Just as different people have different caloric requirements and eat different foods, hedgehogs also vary in their food preferences, the amount they eat, their energy requirements, and how fast they metabolize their food. There is no "one meal fits all" that is perfect for *all* hedgehogs. For example, pregnant and lactating hedgehogs may need to triple the amount that they normally eat. Growing youngsters, adults, old, sick, or debilitated hedgehogs all have different nutritional needs.

The best way to know if you are fulfilling your hedgehog's nutritional requirements is to make sure he is healthy and active, check that he is eating and drinking normally, and weigh him weekly to ensure that he is not too thin and not overweight.

An accurate scale is essential to help you adjust and customize your hedgehog's diet according to his individual needs. Postal scales and food scales are good options because they are sensitive enough to weigh tiny amounts (so you can measure your pet's food or weigh new-born hedgehogs) and can also weigh adult hedgehogs.

African pygmy hedgehogs were originally classified as insectivores, but as previously discussed, their classification has changed. Hedgehogs are actually omnivores. They eat a wide variety of foods, including meat (even carrion) and plants (vegetables and fruits). Hedgehogs enjoy insects, but insects should not make up the majority of their diet. Insects are low in calcium. Some insects are high in fat, especially grubs and waxworms. In addition, not all hedgehogs will eat fruits or vegetables. Hedgehogs are *not* vegetarians and should never be fed a vegetarian diet. Hedgehogs need high-quality protein from animal sources. In fact, recent research suggests that hedgehogs' meals should be high in protein (22 percent), low in fat, and contain adequate fiber (15 percent). Fiber is usually obtained from plant material and insects.

Some hedgehogs develop "food preferences," depending on the taste, and possibly the shape, size, and consistency, of the food. These finicky eaters may eat only their favorite foods and reject other foods they are offered. As a result, these animals may not eat a nutritionally balanced diet. To help prevent this problem, offer your hedgehog a wide variety of foods at an early age (starting during weaning, if possible) so that your pet can become accustomed to different foods and be more likely to accept them.

Commercial Hedgehog Diets

A high-quality commercial hedgehog diet should make up the main part of your hedgehog's diet. It should be high in quality protein (at least 22 percent), low in fat, contain adequate fiber (15 percent), and be low in iron content. The commercial diet should contain high-quality poultry or meat protein. Ingredients are listed on labels in order of the amount, so be sure poultry or meat protein is the first ingredient listed. Avoid diets that consist primarily of grain or corn, or that contain nuts (especially peanuts) or seeds. These can pose a choking or obstruction hazard and are also high in fat. Avoid diets that are fish-based or high in salt.

Before commercial hedgehog foods were available, countless hedgehogs were raised on a combination of kitten or cat food, both growth and maintenance formulas, in canned and dry forms. Often, dog food was added to the mix, although some dog food brands appear to contribute to obesity in hedgehogs.

Over the years, most veterinarians and hedgehog breeders came to the conclusion that cat, kitten, and dog foods do not cover all of a hedgehog's nutritional needs. In addition, these foods contain artificial colors, flavor additives, and preservatives, and are high in fat and salt. Corn is often a key ingredient in dog and cat foods, making them high in carbohydrates, which can lead to obesity.

You can buy commercial hedgehog diet formulations in pet stores or online. Like all commercial pet foods, some formulations are better than others. Ask your veterinarian, hedgehog breeder, and local pet store which commercial hedgehog diets they recommend.

Always check the label to make sure the product is fresh and that its shelf life has not expired. When food is old, vitamins and other nutrients lose their potency.

Hedgehogs don't eat much, so if you have only one or a few hedgehogs, purchase food in small quantities. That way the food won't get old, moldy, rancid, or lose nutritional value before your pet can eat it all.

Fresh Fruits and Vegetables

Fresh fruits (not canned or dried) and fresh vegetables add flavor, nutrition, vitamins, and fiber to your pet's diet, but they should make up only a small part of the diet. Many hedgehogs refuse to eat fruits or vegetables. Offer your hedgehog a wide variety to learn which foods he prefers. Cut fruits and vegetables into very small pieces to make them easier for your hedgehog to eat.

Dog, Cat, and Kitten Food

Today, many hedgehog owners still feed their hedgehogs cat food (sometimes supplemented with dog food), along with small amounts of

fresh fruits, vegetables, and insects. Ideally, these cat and dog foods should be high in quality protein (meat protein, not meal or by-products). Chicken protein is the protein of choice, as lamb is fattening. Cat food contains taurine, a necessary amino acid for cats to help in digestion and protect vision and heart muscles. Some researchers think that taurine may be beneficial for hedgehogs as well, and some commercial hedgehog diets now include taurine.

Although dry cat and dog foods have been credited with helping to reduce tartar accumulation on the teeth, hard foods also tend to wear down tiny hedgehog teeth.

Ferret Food

Some veterinarians recommend that ferret food be included in a hedgehog's diet because ferret food is high in protein (up to 38 percent).

Unfortunately, ferret food is also high in fat (up to 18 percent) and low in fiber (about 4 percent), so it is not a nutritionally balanced food for hedgehogs. Ferret food is concentrated nutrition and high in calories, so a little goes a long way and too much can lead to obesity. However, a small amount of high-quality ferret food added to the diet may prove useful in certain situations, such as helping underweight, stressed, sick, or debilitated animals recover and regain condition.

Insects

Insects are a fun food to give your hedgehog as treats, to supplement the diet, and for environmental enrichment to add to foraging enjoyment. Just be sure that the insects are raised commercially, so they are not exposed to pesticides, toxins, and parasites like insects you trap outside might be. Commercially raised insects (crickets, mealworms, waxworms) are available live, or in freeze-dried form. Feed insects in moderation. Insects are low in calcium and some are high in fat.

How Much and How Often

African pygmy hedgehogs are eager eaters. Some can be true gluttons, so it's up to you to keep track of how much your pet eats and not overfeed him!

On average, your hedgehog will eat 1 to 3 tablespoons of food daily, depending on his size, activity level, age, health, and the type of diet being fed. That might not seem like very much food, but your pet is very small and so is his stomach. Hedgehogs can't eat enough food in one meal to cover their nutritional needs for a 24-hour period. Most hedgehogs need to have two daily meals to meet their needs.

African pygmy hedgehogs are most active in the evening and early morning. To keep in step with your pet's natural schedule, give the main meal in the evening and give a light meal in the early morning if he is still hungry. Remove uneaten food after the morning meal, so that it doesn't spoil.

Do not leave food out for your hedgehog all the time (free-choice feeding), except in special circumstances such as pregnancy or lactation, or if your pet is underweight or ill.

Menu for Hedgehogs

Individual hedgehogs have their own nutritional requirements, according to their age, health, activity level, sex, and reproductive status. Research suggests that African pygmy hedgehogs in captivity need 70 to 100 calories daily.

A *high-quality* commercially formulated complete hedgehog diet should be the main component of your pet's meals whenever possible. This can be supplemented with a few live insects and a small quantity of fresh fruits and vegetables daily. You can also add a small amount of cooked egg or finely cut cooked meat. If your hedgehog is not lactose intolerant, you can add a small amount of low-fat cottage cheese to the diet.

If you cannot find a suitable commercial hedgehog formulation, the following *guideline* for hedgehog meals is offered:

1. One-quarter to one-half teaspoon finely chopped fresh fruits (apple, pear, melon)

2. One-quarter to one-half teaspoon finely chopped fresh vegetables (carrots, peas, leafy greens). You may sometimes substitute vegetable blend, or vegetable and poultry blend, baby food (without onions) for humans.

3. One-quarter to one-half teaspoon cooked skinless chicken breast or cooked egg

4. One-quarter teaspoon low-fat cottage cheese

5. One teaspoon high-quality cat food

6. One-quarter teaspoon high-quality dog food

Add four to six tiny mealworms or one to two small crickets or one newborn "pinky" mouse purchased frozen from pet store.

Important:

✔ Weigh your hedgehog once a week and adjust his diet accordingly.

✔ Wash all fruits and vegetables well before feeding them to your pet, to remove bacteria and pesticides.

✔ Hedgehogs are not vegetarians. If your pet refuses to eat fruits and vegetables, increase the portion size of other ingredients accordingly.

Additional hedgehog meal suggestions can be found in the *Exotic Companion Medicine Handbook* (see "Information").

Vitamins, Minerals, and Supplements

If your hedgehog is receiving a high-quality commercial hedgehog or cat food diet, it is not usually necessary to supplement the diet with vitamins and minerals unless your veterinarian recommends that you do so. Indiscriminate supplementation can be harmful.

Hedgehog Feeding Tips

1. Ask your veterinarian to help you formulate a balanced diet for your hedgehog.

2. Examine your hedgehog daily to make sure he is healthy, eating, and drinking.

3. Measure your pet's food and keep track of how much he eats and drinks.

4. Weigh your hedgehog weekly to make sure he is maintaining a good weight for his size.

5. Feed your hedgehog in the evening and early morning when he is active.

6. To prevent obesity, do not feed your hedgehog ad lib or free choice.

7. Do not overfeed your hedgehog.

8. If your hedgehog is overweight, don't put him on a "crash diet" or rapid food reduction diet. Decrease your pet's caloric intake by *gradually* limiting the amount you feed him and by cutting back on foods high in fats. Increasing the fiber content of your pet's diet may also help.

9. Never change your hedgehog's diet suddenly. If a food change is needed, make the change *gradually* to prevent gastrointestinal upset, diarrhea, and illness. A sudden change of diet and illness can cause green, unformed, foul-smelling feces.

10. Do not feed your hedgehog a vegetarian diet. This could lead to serious health problems and nutritional deficiencies.

11. Many hedgehogs will not eat if they do not have a safe and secure place to sleep.

12. *Adjust your hedgehog's diet according to his activity level, health, reproductive status, age, and needs.*

Your hedgehog is overweight if he

1. cannot roll up completely into a tight ball,

2. has fat under his chin (looks like a "double chin"), or

3. has extra fat under his front legs (in the axillary "armpit" areas).

Feeding with a Syringe or Eyedropper

At some time you may be faced with the challenge of feeding your hedgehog by hand, using a syringe or eyedropper, to help him survive. For example, if you have baby hedgehogs that are orphaned or have been neglected or abandoned by their mother, you will have to feed them by hand until they are weaned. If you have an adult hedgehog that is too sick or weak to eat on his own, he will have to be fed with a syringe until he recovers.

Feeding with a syringe or eyedropper must be done very carefully. Before you begin, ask your veterinarian for help in

✔ estimating the size of your hedgehog's stomach and how much it can hold;

✔ determining if your hedgehog is dehydrated; and

✔ learning how to feed using a syringe, eyedropper, or tiny stomach tube.

How to Feed Using a Syringe or Eyedropper

Use a 1 milliliter (1 cc or Tuberculin) syringe, or an eyedropper that dispenses in tiny drops. Wrap your hedgehog in a soft cloth and hold him securely and comfortably in one hand. With the other hand, place the tip of the syringe gently against his mouth, lips, or tongue and feed him slowly, drop by drop. Make sure each drop is swallowed before feeding the next drop.

What to Feed Baby Hedgehogs

Baby hedgehogs can be successfully raised on Esbilac, a puppy milk replacer available from pet stores and veterinarians. Do not use kitten milk replacers (too high in fat), milk replacers for human babies, or cow's milk (these do not adequately meet the needs of baby hedgehogs and can cause diarrhea). Tiny meals warmed to body temperature and given at frequent intervals are critical for success.

After eating, a baby hedgehog must be stimulated to urinate and defecate. Take a soft cotton ball moistened in warm water and very gently dab (don't rub!) the baby's belly in the direction from just under the rib cage toward the pelvis region. This simulates a mother hedgehog's tongue licking. Dry the baby's belly by gently dabbing it with a soft cloth.

Baby hedgehogs that are not drinking mother's milk will have unusually colored feces, ranging from yellowish to dark green in color. The feces may also have an abnormal odor and consistency (pasty, loose, or constipated). When the babies are weaned to a high-quality commercial diet, their feces will return to normal brown-black color, semi-dry consistency, volume, and odor.

What to Feed Sick, Weak Adult Hedgehogs

Esbilac can be used for syringe feeding sick or weak hedgehogs. You might also try the author's hospital formulation (below) to help your pet's recovery. This formulation is *not* for hedgehogs that are not yet weaned.

Feeding Guidelines

✔ *Feed very small, frequent meals and feed them very slowly.* A few mouthfuls per meal is sufficient to start. Newborn hedgehogs can be fed 0.1 to 0.2 ml of formula every 1.5 to 2 hours. As the baby grows, slowly increase its food intake. Adult hedgehogs may consume 1 ml of formula every 2 hours. Depending on the animal's size, condition, and appetite, more may be required.

✔ *Do not overfeed.* If your pet is fed more than his stomach can hold, he will regurgitate the food and can aspirate it into his trachea and lungs. If this happens, it is almost impossible to save your hedgehog from death by suffocation or aspiration pneumonia.

Hedgehog Recovery Diet

Two newborn "pinky" mice (purchased frozen from the pet store)
8 small mealworms
1½ ounce (45 ml) Esbilac
1 teaspoonful (5 ml) Pedialyte

Using a blender, mix well into a smooth liquid. Using 3 ml syringes, draw up into portions of 1, 2, or 3 ml (as desired) each and freeze all portions.

Thaw each portion at room temperature. Warm syringe in your hand and feed immediately when formula is warm. *Discard any leftovers.*

✔ *Feed your hedgehog very slowly.* To prevent your pet from inhaling the formula into his lungs, feed one small drop at a time and make sure it is swallowed before giving another drop.

✔ *Make sure your hedgehog is warm before you feed him.* Chilled animals may suffer from temporary abnormal inactivity of the gut, and feeding a small, chilled animal may kill it.

✔ *Make sure your hedgehog is not dehydrated before you feed him.* Feeding formula to a dehydrated animal may make the problem worse. You can give your hedgehog small amounts of Pedialyte solution, or you can make the first meal a mixture of half Esbilac and half Pedialyte solution.

✔ *Listen to your hedgehog!* Baby hedgehogs make soft peeps when they are hungry.

Potentially Harmful Foods

1. Mealworms, crickets, or other insects that are wild, dead, or decayed may carry bacteria that can make your hedgehog sick.

2. Foods high in sugar (dried fruits) or fat can lead to obesity, dental problems, and other health problems.

3. Foods that are sharp, dry, stiff, or sticky (such as candy, raisins, peanuts, popcorn, dried fruits) can lodge in the mouth, throat, or gastrointestinal tract and cause choking or intestinal obstruction.

4. Foods manufactured for rodents are nutritionally deficient for hedgehogs. Also, hedgehogs are unable to remove seed shells and may choke on the seeds.

5. Raw meat and raw eggs can contain disease-causing bacteria, such as *Salmonella*.

6. Chocolate contains theobromine, a product similar to caffeine, which has been shown to be toxic for some animals (chocolate is toxic for dogs).

7. Dairy products may cause diarrhea. After weaning, many hedgehogs lose their ability to digest milk and become lactose (milk sugar) intolerant.

8. Corn is fattening and can cause allergies and skin problems in some animals.

9. Some vegetables cause problems in other species and, to be safe, should not be fed to hedgehogs. Onions are toxic to cats. Broccoli, cauliflower, peppers, and similar vegetables cause gas production or intestinal upset in some species and are not recommended for hedgehogs. Do not feed your hedgehog the green parts, sprouts, or "eyes" of potatoes. These contain a toxin called *solanine*.

Note: Grapes and raisins can cause severe kidney failure and death in dogs. If grapes have an adverse effect on hedgehog kidneys, it has not yet been documented, but the possibility should be considered when planning your pet's diet.

If you are not sure about the safety or nutritional benefit of any food type, do not feed it to your hedgehog!

Water

African pygmy hedgehogs should have access to pure, clean drinking water at all times. Factors that increase thirst and the need for water include a dry diet, warm weather, low humidity, pregnancy, lactation (milk production), and health problems (such as kidney disease, diarrhea, and diabetes). *Always provide more water than your hedgehog normally drinks.*

The best water you can give your hedgehog is the same drinking water you filter or buy for yourself. City or well water may contain addi-

tives, undesirable elements, or bacteria. Do not give your pet distilled, de-mineralized, de-ionized, or carbonated water. Commercial bottled purified or spring drinking water is an inexpensive and safe way to keep your hedgehog healthy and hydrated.

Water intake varies among individual animals based on their size, age, activity level, diet, health status, reproductive activity, and environmental conditions. If your hedgehog is pregnant or nursing babies, she may drink two to three times or more of the amount of water she usually does.

If you have baby hedgehogs, lower their water bottle so that the sipper tube is easily within their reach, above the cage bedding.

Baby hedgehogs are active. As they wander about the cage, bedding is moved about and may eventually become higher in some areas of the cage than others. Check frequently to see that the sipper tube is not plugged and that water has not leaked into the bedding.

If your hedgehog is not drinking enough, or is drinking excessively, this can indicate a health problem, so contact your veterinarian immediately.

Nutritional Disorders

The most common nutritional disorders in hedgehogs are obesity and fatty liver disease (hepatic lipidosis).

HEALTH

The most important health care you can give your hedgehog is preventive health care. Preventing problems is much easier than treating problems. Some problems cannot be prevented, but if you detect them early and treat them immediately, your hedgehog has a much better chance of recovery. Check your hedgehog every day!

Hedgehogs are hardy little animals. With excellent care and a balanced, nutritious diet your hedgehog may live several years. But if your hedgehog becomes ill, he will need immediate help from your veterinarian and lots of care and attention from you. This chapter gives you the information you need to know about hedgehog health problems, how to recognize them, what to do about them, and how to keep your hedgehog healthy.

Keeping Your Hedgehog Healthy

It is a natural survival instinct for wild animals to be stoic and hide their pains and illnesses as well as possible, so that they do not appear weak and vulnerable to predators. That is why it is often difficult to know when your hedgehog is sick until the illness has progressed to the point that your pet can no longer hide

it. By that time, treatment may be difficult and less likely to succeed.

Signs of a Sick Hedgehog

Even the best-cared-for hedgehogs can become sick. Successful recovery depends upon the health problem the hedgehog has, how early it was noticed, and how quickly it was diagnosed and treated. *Sick hedgehogs rarely recover without immediate help and treatment.*

If your pet is weak or lethargic; is losing large numbers of quills; cannot maintain a normal stance or posture; is unable to walk normally; is not eating or drinking; is losing weight; has discharge from the eyes, ears, or mouth; or has diarrhea or constipation, then your hedgehog needs help immediately.

Sick hedgehogs can be very difficult to examine. They may be in pain, stressed or frightened, and more prone to biting. If your hedgehog curls into a ball, it will be almost

Is Your Hedgehog Healthy?

	Healthy Hedgehog	Sick Hedgehog
Appearance	Bright, clear eyes	Dull expression; eyes irritated, or with discharge; eyes partially closed; protruding eyes
	Clean ears	Debris around ears and in ear canals; discharge from ears
	Clean nose and nostrils	Nasal discharge, swelling, or bleeding
	Clean quills and fur; healthy skin	Excessive quill loss; bald areas between quills; piles of dander and debris in skin or at base of quills; visible external parasites; red, swollen, irritated skin; abnormal lumps, bumps, or growths; soiled or irritated skin around anus and genital area; penile sheath matted or plugged with debris; signs of diarrhea
	Normal teeth and gums	Drooling; foul odor from mouth; excessive tartar accumulation on teeth; red or swollen gums; blood or pus in mouth; swollen jaws; painful mouth; reluctance to eat; dropping food from mouth when attempting to eat
	Robust, compact body	Thin and losing weight, or excessive weight gain, or obesity
Behavior	Alert, active, curious	Lethargic, depressed, slow, reclusive
	Good appetite and drinking	Poor appetite; not eating or drinking
	Breathes normally	Difficulty breathing; wheezing, sneezing, coughing, choking
	Wanders, forages, explores, climbs, and runs in exercise wheel; curls in ball in defense; snorts, jumps, and butts with head when startled; spreads saliva on his quills when encountering new objects and smells	Lethargic; abnormal body position; abnormal stance or gait; head tilt, excessive scratching; continual circling; repetitive biting at cage bars; loss of balance; paralysis

impossible to examine him until he relaxes. On the other hand, if your pet is too weak to curl into a ball, his condition is very serious.

Possible Signs of Pain
1. Loss of appetite
2. Reluctance to move
3. Lameness
4. Sudden defensive behavior
5. Unusually sensitive to touch
6. Half-closed, dull eyes
7. Loss of interest in surroundings
8. Dropping food out of mouth
9. Inability to curl up into a ball
10. Unusual vocalization when touched or handled

If Your Hedgehog Is Sick

1. Isolate your pet in a comfortable, quiet area with subdued lighting, to reduce stress. Keep your hedgehog away from other pets, to keep him safe and to reduce the chances of spreading illness if the problem is contagious.

2. Contact your veterinarian immediately. An examination is necessary to accurately diagnose the condition. A prescription medication may be needed to ensure your pet's survival.

3. To prevent the possible spread of infectious disease, wash your hands thoroughly after handling your sick hedgehog and before handling other pets or food. Wash all housing, accessories, exercise wheels, dishes, and bottles that were in contact with your sick pet and discard soiled bedding.

4. Sick hedgehogs are easily stressed when they are transported. Some veterinarians make house calls, but if they cannot bring the special equipment they need to examine and treat a

TIP

Emergency Care
In an emergency, you can find electrolyte solutions (such as Pedialyte) formulated for human babies at pharmacies and grocery stores. Keep a bottle on hand for your hedgehog in case of emergency.

Never give your hedgehog homemade salt mixtures. In the wrong proportions, these mixtures can worsen your pet's condition.

hedgehog in your home, you will have to take your pet to the veterinary clinic. To reduce stress, transport your hedgehog in a travel kennel covered with a light blanket or towel to reduce sounds and light.

Helping Your Veterinarian Help You

Hedgehogs are challenging patients. They differ in many ways from common domestic pet species. Ideally, you have chosen a veterinarian who has experience and expertise with hedgehogs.

To make the most of your pet's visit to the veterinarian, prepare a list of the questions you want to ask the doctor. Your veterinarian will also ask you several questions about your pet to better understand the case, such as the following:

✔ Where did you obtain or purchase your hedgehog?
✔ How long have you owned your pet?
✔ How old is your hedgehog?

✔ Is it spayed or neutered?

✔ If your hedgehog is a female, is she pregnant, or has she ever produced a litter?

✔ Describe housing, handling, and exercise routines.

✔ What do you feed your hedgehog? How much do you feed, including treats and supplements?

✔ Are there any other animals at home? If you have other hedgehogs, do they have similar problems?

✔ Has your pet been exposed to any sick animals or harmful chemicals?

✔ When did you first notice the problem?

✔ Does your pet appear to be in any discomfort or pain?

✔ What, if anything, have you given or done to treat the problem?

✔ When did your hedgehog last eat or drink?

This sick hedgehog is lethargic, drooling, and is unable to stand or curl into a ball.

✔ Has there been a change in your hedgehog's diet or living environment?

✔ When did your hedgehog last defecate and urinate?

✔ Does your hedgehog have normal stools, or constipation, or diarrhea?

✔ Has your hedgehog lost or gained weight?

Don't worry if you don't have all the answers. Any information you give your veterinarian will be helpful.

Health Problems

Hedgehogs can contract or carry bacterial, viral, and fungal infections. They can also be infested with several types of internal parasites. Skin problems caused by external parasites, especially mites, are common in hedgehogs. Hedgehogs can also suffer from noncontagious medical conditions, such as trauma, obesity, heart problems, heatstroke, neurological problems (including Wobbly Hedgehog Syndrome), and cancer.

Most hedgehogs are healthy, hardy animals when they receive good care and nutrition. The following discussion and list of possible hedgehog health problems may seem very long. Don't let this list frighten or discourage you. Use this information to your advantage to recognize health problems in your hedgehog as soon as they occur, so you can give immediate first aid when possible.

If your hedgehog has any of the medical conditions listed in this chapter, you should contact your veterinarian immediately.

Anorexia

Anorexia is loss of appetite or refusal to eat. Some hedgehogs stop eating when they are stressed, in pain, when their environment or food has been changed, or during breeding. Anorexia can also indicate a serious health problem, such as dental disease, cancer, a drop in temperature (both ambient and body), parasitism (internal or external), or infections.

Treatment: Keep your hedgehog comfortable and warm. Encourage eating and feed with a syringe or eyedropper, if necessary.

Bite Wounds

Hedgehogs can interact aggressively, especially males or breeding pairs, or animals that are in close confinement, stressed, or overcrowded, and do not have enough hideaways to avoid each other. During these agitated encounters, hedgehogs may charge, butt heads, growl, squeal, and snort. Hedgehogs seldom bite, but when they do, they can inflict serious wounds that may become infected and form abscesses.

Eliminate the risk of bite wounds by housing hedgehogs individually. Protect your hedgehogs from other animals that can attack and harm them.

To check your hedgehog for bite wounds, check between the quills for any lumps, bumps, punctures, cuts, lacerations, bleeding, swelling, redness, tenderness, abscesses, or pus. A deep bite wound can cause muscle and nerve damage, or fracture your hedgehog's delicate bones.

Treatment: Clean the wound with a mild antiseptic solution or antibacterial soap and water. Your veterinarian may prescribe oral antibiotics as well as antibiotic ointments to apply to the wound. Keep the wound clean and allow it to drain until it has healed.

Cancer

Cancer is very common among pet hedgehogs, especially those more than three years of age. Several types of cancer have been identified in African pgymy hedgehogs. The more common types of cancer are mammary tumors, gastrointestinal tumors, lymphosarcoma, tumors of the mouth, and skin tumors. More than 65 percent of hedgehog cancer cases are malignant. In one study, 29 percent of hedgehogs necropsied (examination of internal organs after death) had cancer. There are many causes of cancer in hedgehogs, including retroviruses.

Cardiomyopathy

Heart muscle disease is common in pet hedgehogs. In one study, 38 percent of hedgehogs necropsied had some form of cardiomyopathy.

Dehydration

Dehydration occurs when an animal loses too much fluid from the body. There are many causes of dehydration, including not drinking enough water, illness, diarrhea, vomiting, and a hot, dry environment.

Treatment: The treatment for dehydration is to rehydrate (replenish the body with water). It may be difficult to tell if your hedgehog is dehydrated, but if he has been exposed to high temperatures or overheated, he is likely dehydrated. Encourage your hedgehog to drink, but do not force water intake if your pet is unconscious or too weak to drink on his own. Forcing your hedgehog to drink could cause him to aspirate water into his lungs, leading to respiratory problems.

Your veterinarian may give your hedgehog fluids and electrolytes by injection.

Dental Problems

Dental problems are very common in hedgehogs. Some problems include excessive tartar

accumulation, gum and periodontal disease, infections, tooth root abscesses, diseases of the jawbone, osteomyelitis (bone inflammation), trauma, and cancer. Hedgehogs must be sedated to thoroughly examine their teeth, because a hedgehog's mouth is difficult to examine and many dental problems are painful.

Signs of dental disease include reluctance to eat, lack of appetite, drooling, dropping food when eating, foul odor from mouth, excessive tartar accumulation on teeth, red or swollen gums, bleeding from the mouth, swollen jaws, and pain.

Treatment: Your veterinarian should check your hedgehog's teeth at least once a year and clean and polish them as needed. Some hedgehogs need dental cleaning every six months and some need to have extractions, especially if the roots of the teeth are abscessed. In these cases, antibiotics and pain medications are prescribed.

Ear Disease

Ear problems can be caused by parasites, infection, or injury. Most hedgehog ear diseases are caused by parasitic mites (*Chorioptes* and *Notoedres* species, and *Caparinia tripilis*). Mites are not easily seen with the naked eye. They are found around the ears, on the head, and at the base of the quills, and cause excessive dander.

Signs of ear problems include scratching at the ears (although some hedgehogs with ear mites may not scratch), crusty skin lesions on the margins and tips of the ears, head shaking, tilting the head to one side (usually to the affected side), loss of balance, and in severe cases, loss of hearing. Hearing loss can also be caused by debris buildup plugging the ear canals. When the debris is removed, hearing returns. Hedgehogs rely heavily on their keen hearing, and ear disease can be very painful, so it is important to take care of ear problems as soon as they are discovered.

Treatment: Place a drop of mineral oil on a cotton-tipped swab and gently wipe away any dirt or debris from your hedgehog's ears. This may give your pet some temporary relief from itching until you can take your hedgehog to your veterinarian for a diagnosis and prescription medication. Do not push the swab into the ear canal!

Eye Problems

Eye problems can develop from injury, infection, or irritating substances. Check your hedgehog's eyes daily to be sure they are clear and bright. If your hedgehog's eyes are dull, cloudy, have a discharge, or are partially closed, place your pet in a dark room. Injured eyes are very painful and sensitive to light. Contact your veterinarian immediately for diagnosis and treatment.

African pygmy hedgehogs can suffer from proptosis. This means that the eye has come out of the socket and that the eyelids are behind the protruding eye instead of in front of the eye. Blindness results, and unless treated immediately, the eye must be surgically removed. Reported cases of proptosis in African pygmy hedgehogs involved one or both eyes (one eye in most cases). The exact cause of proptosis is not known, but studied cases suggest that African pygmy hedgehogs may be predisposed (prone) to the condition for several reasons:

1. The hedgehog's eye is relatively large (measured at 0.23 inches [6 mm]) in relation to the shallow eye socket (measured at 0.04 inches [1 mm]).

2. Eyelid conformation may be a contributing cause, as the eyelids open wide, making it easier for the eye to protrude.

3. Fat behind the eyeball makes the eye socket shallower and allows less room for the eyeball. So, obese hedgehogs may have an increased risk of proptosis because of excess fat behind the eye.

4. Researchers noted that proptosis can also be caused by eye socket inflammation and swelling, usually from foreign objects penetrating the eye and causing bacterial infection, or dental root infections, or trauma.

As a preventive measure to protect the remaining eye in hedgehogs that have already lost one eye, researchers suggested partially sewing the eyelids together to narrow the opening as an option.

Of special note, some of the hedgehogs that suffered from proptosis also had neurological problems.

Hedgehogs do not have good eyesight and rely mostly on their senses of smell, hearing, and touch. They are able to survive and adapt in captivity without their eyesight, if special care is taken.

Fatty Liver Disease (Hepatic Lipidosis)

Fatty liver disease is one of the most common and serious health problems seen in captive, obese hedgehogs. It is caused by excessive fat accumulation in the liver, leading to abnormal liver function. When the liver does not work properly, it cannot clear toxins from the body.

Hedgehogs suffering from fatty liver disease are lethargic, lose interest in food, eventually lose weight, and can die. Hedgehogs with "sudden death" may actually have been suffering from fatty liver disease.

Fatty liver disease is diagnosed by laboratory tests, ultrasound imaging, and, if necessary, liver biopsy. To help prevent your pet from developing fatty liver disease, do not overfeed him. Give your hedgehog a balanced, low-fat diet with sufficient fiber, and make sure he gets plenty of exercise.

Gastrointestinal Disease

Stomach and intestinal problems can be caused by bacterial or viral infections, internal parasites, incorrect diet, stress, unsanitary housing conditions, foreign bodies, and cancer. Signs of gastrointestinal problems include lack of appetite, vomiting, lethargy, weight loss, constipation, or diarrhea.

Note: Normal feces are brown or black in color, firm, and semi-dry. *If your hedgehog has not produced feces for 24 hours, if his feces are green or loose, or if there is blood or mucus in the feces, contact your veterinarian immediately.*

Constipation

Constipation is difficulty passing dry, hard feces. Causes of constipation include dehydration, insufficient water intake, dry or hot environment, obstruction of the intestinal tract (foreign objects, hair), and parasitism. If your hedgehog is very relaxed, you might be able to feel the hard, lumpy fecal material in his abdomen.

Treatment: Be sure your hedgehog has fresh water available in the bottle at all times and is drinking. Add a water dish to your pet's enclosure to encourage drinking. Remove all dry food and replace it with moist food until the stools return to normal.

Diarrhea

Diarrhea has many causes, including infection, parasitism, stress, and incorrect diet. If not treated quickly, diarrhea can cause rapid dehydration and even death. The feces may be foul smelling, green in color, mucus-like, or liquid. The area around the anus may be red, swollen, irritated, and soiled.

Treatment: Diarrhea must be diagnosed and treated immediately. Your pet may need medication to stop the diarrhea, as well as fluids to treat dehydration.

Intestinal Obstruction

Intestinal obstruction is a painful, life-threatening condition. Signs include vomiting, lack of appetite, lethargy, dehydration, and weight loss. Emergency surgery is usually necessary.

Intestinal Parasites

Hedgehogs can be infested by several types of intestinal parasites. They include roundworms (such as whipworms and pinworms), tapeworms, and protozoa.

Intestinal parasites can cause severe illness, weight loss, and diarrhea. Take a fresh fecal (stool) sample to your veterinarian to check under the microscope for the presence of parasites and their eggs. Accurate identification of the offending parasite is important and will determine the type of medication your veterinarian prescribes. Not all kinds of medications work for all types of internal parasites, so parasite identification is necessary to treat your hedgehog successfully and safely.

Heatstroke

Hedgehogs can become overheated and suffer from heatstroke. Be sure that your hedge-

hog's housing is not in direct sunlight and is not close to heat sources. House your pet in an area with comfortable temperature control and adequate ventilation.

If you must transport your hedgehog, never leave him in the car, not even for a very short time. On a warm day, the inside of a car can heat up to 120°F (49°C) in a few minutes, even with the windows partially open.

If your hedgehog is exposed to high temperatures, he will quickly become weak, unresponsive, and comatose. Without immediate emergency treatment he will die. You must act quickly to safely lower your hedgehog's temperature. Then you will have to rehydrate your pet. Your pet's normal core body temperature is 97–99°F (36–37°C).

Treatment: To cool down your hedgehog, hold him in your hands in a sink of cool (not cold) water. Be sure to keep your pet's head above water so he can breathe. When your pet is cooled down, dry him gently. Observe your hedgehog to make sure he regains consciousness, and then place him in a dry, dark, comfortable cage to rest. Your hedgehog will need fluids. Before offering him water, make sure he is fully conscious and able to swallow so that he does not aspirate fluid into his lungs. Give your hedgehog a dish to encourage drinking, in case he is too weak to reach the sipper tube. Consult your veterinarian immediately for follow-up treatment, including fluid therapy, and medications to prevent brain swelling, shock, and other problems caused by heatstroke.

Infections

Infections and infectious diseases are caused by bacteria, viruses, fungi, and protozoa. Symptoms vary and include lack of appetite, weight loss, and lethargy or inactivity. Severe infections can lead to death. Consult your veterinarian immediately for diagnosis and treatment.

Injury

Hedgehogs sometimes are in the wrong place at the wrong time. Your home can be a hazardous place for a hapless hedgehog. If your pet climbs and falls, is dropped, stepped on, attacked

by another animal, or injured in any way, the damage to your tiny friend could be very serious.

If your hedgehog has been injured, examine him closely, but do not handle him more than necessary. Place your hedgehog in a quiet, dark area to reduce stress until you can reach your veterinarian.

Kidney (Renal) Disease

Kidney disease is a serious, debilitating condition in which the kidneys fail to function properly. It is very common in African pygmy hedgehogs. In one study, 50 percent of hedgehogs necropsied had renal disease.

Renal disease causes weight loss and increased thirst and urination, and eventually ends in death.

Neurological Problems

Vestibular Disease (Vestibular Syndrome)

Located in the inner ear, adjacent to hearing receptors, is the vestibular system. The vestibular system helps animals keep their balance and coordinate eye movement by sensing the posi-

tion of the head and body in relation to space, movement, and gravity. Information from the vestibular system is processed in the brain.

Vestibular disease is characterized by loss of coordination, dizziness, nausea, vomiting, head tilt (usually to the affected side), and in severe cases, falling over or rolling over to one side. Nystagmus is common in vestibular disease. Nystagmus is abnormal, rapid rhythmic movement of the eyes, up and down or side to side (as in left to right).

In most cases, vestibular disease in hedgehogs has a sudden onset and lasts a few to several days. In some cases vestibular disease can be caused by infection of the middle ear. Vestibular disease can also have more serious causes, such as tumors or injury.

Wobbly Hedgehog Syndrome (WHS)

Wobbly Hedgehog Syndrome (WHS) is a serious neurological condition that is seen most commonly in hedgehogs less than two years of age, although animals of any age can be affected. The disease causes lack of muscle coordination and difficulty balancing. As the hedgehog loses coordination and balance, he wobbles, trips, stumbles, falls, and has difficulty eating from dishes. The condition gradually worsens over time, until the hedgehog falls over repeatedly (to the same side) and cannot right himself. The sick animal will make running movements while lying on his side. Tremors may develop into seizures. Affected hedgehogs may also have difficulty swallowing. In more than a quarter of the cases of WHS in one study, the hedgehogs also had abnormal protrusion of one eye. In about 70 percent of the cases, paralysis started with the hind limbs and gradually advanced to the forelimbs. The paralysis may be one-sided in the beginning, but eventually spreads to both sides of the body. The hedgehog is eventually unable to eat from dishes, continues to lose weight, and must be hand-fed with a syringe or eyedropper. Some hedgehogs can be kept alive for several months with dedicated nursing care, but all cases end in death. Some published case studies say that approximately 10 percent of pet African pygmy hedgehogs become affected with the disorder. A similar condition has been documented in European hedgehogs. To date there is no treatment for this devastating disease, which is currently believed to be genetically inherited.

Other neurological problems may be confused with WHS, but a diagnosis of WHS can be confirmed by the microscopic study of the animal's brain and spinal cord.

Respiratory Problems

Respiratory problems, especially pneumonia, are among the most common hedgehog health problems. Some respiratory problems are caused by fine, powdery materials that can irritate the hedgehog's respiratory tract. *Pneumonia is caused by infectious agents and is life threatening.* Bacterial infections (*Bordetella bronchiseptica, Pasteurella multocida*), *Mycoplasma*, or viral infections take hold while the animal is weakened or stressed. Respiratory problems can be triggered when the hedgehog becomes chilled, or is left in a cold, drafty, damp, or dirty environment, as stress makes it more susceptible to infection. If you hear your hedgehog wheezing, snuffling, or sneezing, or if he has labored breathing, get immediate veterinary care. Your veterinarian may recommend oxygen therapy, antibiotics, rest, and isolation in a warm incubator.

Signs of pneumonia include breathing difficulty, discharge from the eyes and nose, lack of appetite, inactivity, and weight loss.

Skin Disease and Quill Loss

Signs of skin and quill problems include excessive dander; dry, flaky, itchy skin; reddened skin; sores; and quill loss. Skin disease is the most common hedgehog problem seen in veterinary practices, and most cases are caused by mites. The Psoroptid mite, *Caparinia tripilis*, is a common hedgehog parasite. The parasite clusters on the skin of the head, ears, flanks, and inside of legs. Mild infestations may go unnoticed, but heavier infestations cause severe quill loss and dry, flaky, thickened, folded skin that cracks and bleeds and can become infected. In addition, skin fungus, such as ringworm (*Trichophyton mentagrophytes* var. *erinacei*), can infiltrate the skin, making the condition worse. Heavy infestations around the eyes can lead to lesions and blindness. Severe infestations can cause debilitation and death. *Chorioptes* mites are visible around the base of the quills. *Sarcoptes* mites live under the skin, so are more difficult to diagnose and eliminate. Skin problems may also be caused by fleas and ticks, improper diet, hormonal imbalance, disease, or bacterial and fungal infections.

Your veterinarian's expertise is necessary to diagnose the exact cause of your pet's condition. Quill and skin scraping samples must be examined under the microscope and cultured for fungal and bacterial growth. Prescription medication is needed, and several treatments may be necessary to treat the problem successfully.

Mighty Mite

The *Caparinia* mite was first recognized in Great Britain as a hedgehog parasite more than a century ago. The mite was introduced from Great Britain into New Zealand in the nineteenth century, riding on the skin of imported hedgehogs. In 1991 the United States placed a ban on the importation of hedgehogs from Africa, because of the risk of transmission of foot-and-mouth disease, which can be carried by hedgehogs and is a serious threat to livestock. For that reason, hedgehogs for breeding stock and pets were then imported into the United States from New Zealand. But the imported hedgehogs brought their parasite, the *Caparinia* mite, along with them, introducing the mite into the United States.

Urogenital Disease

Diseases of the urinary tract and genitals are common in hedgehogs. They include urinary tract infection, bladder stones, uterine bleeding, and cancer. Signs of urogenital disease include difficulty urinating, dark-colored urine, blood in urine, lack of urination, lethargy, lack of appetite, pain, dehydration, decreased or excessive drinking, and vomiting. A veterinary examination is necessary to diagnose and treat the problem. Bladder stones and tumors require surgical removal.

Unavoidable Problems

Some medical conditions cannot be prevented. These include problems with the heart, kidneys, liver, or other internal organs; problems associated with aging or genetics; and cancer. If your hedgehog has a medical problem that cannot be cured, you can still give your pet the best home remedy of all—nutritious food and a safe, comfortable, loving home.

Medications

Veterinarians specializing in exotic animals, wild animals, and nondomestic animals have compiled formularies of medications that they consider safe for hedgehogs.

Give your pet only medicines prescribed by your veterinarian. Give no more than the prescribed dose.

Never give your hedgehog any medicine prescribed for you or your other pets.

Emergency First Aid Kit

✔ Veterinarian's phone number
✔ Phone number of the nearest emergency pet hospital that will accept hedgehog patients (Obtain this information *before* your pet has an emergency!)
✔ Mineral oil
✔ Electrolyte solution (can use Pedialyte, available at grocery store or pharmacy)
✔ Artificial tears
✔ Topical triple antibiotic ointment (without corticosteroids) available from local store without prescription
✔ Gentle antiseptic solution (Hibiclens, Nolvasan)
✔ Small flat, baby nail trimmers

✔ Eyedropper or 1 ml or 3 ml syringe for feeding
✔ Small forceps or tweezers
✔ Magnifying glass
✔ Penlight or small flashlight
✔ Styptic pencil or powder
✔ Cotton-tipped swabs
✔ Clean, small towels (not terry cloth)

Zoonotic Diseases

Zoonotic diseases are diseases that can be shared between animals and humans. Many species of animals are carriers of diseases that do not make them ill but can make people very sick. Likewise, people can carry diseases to which humans are resistant but that make other animal species ill. Some disease organisms cause illness in both humans and animals.

Hedgehogs can carry some zoonotic diseases (bacterial, viral, and fungal). These two are the most common diseases transmitted from hedgehogs to humans:

✔ *Salmonellosis*—a bacterial disease (Approximately one-third of hedgehogs are carriers; however, transmission from hedgehogs to humans is rare.)
✔ *Trichophyton mentagrophytes* var.*erinacei*—a fungal disease ("ringworm")

Disease spread can be prevented by thorough hand washing after handling hedgehogs.

Note: Hedgehogs may be mistakenly thought to have rabies, a fatal viral disease contagious to humans and other mammals, when they ant (hypersalivate, anoint), or if they have a neurological disease.

It is highly unlikely that a pet hedgehog raised in captivity would have rabies unless it has been housed outdoors with exposure to other animals. Although it is unlikely, hedgehogs *can* get rabies. At this time there is not an approved rabies vaccine for hedgehogs.

If your hedgehog is ill, your veterinarian can answer questions you may have about the potential for contagion of different diseases or parasites.

When Surgery Is Necessary

In some cases, surgery may be the only way to treat or save your hedgehog. Fortunately for today's hedgehogs, safer anesthetics and surgical and dental techniques make it possible for veterinarians to successfully perform lifesaving procedures when they are needed.

Your hedgehog might need surgery to
✔ repair an injury or laceration,
✔ biopsy or remove a tumor,
✔ remove an intestinal obstruction,
✔ extract an abscessed tooth,
✔ perform a Caesarian-section, or
✔ remove the reproductive organs (neutering)*.

*Most hedgehogs do not need to be neutered, except for medical reasons, such as infection or cancer.

Home Hospital Cage

You can set up a "hospital cage" to observe your hedgehog while he recovers from surgery. A 30-gallon (115 L) Plexiglas aquarium with a snap-on lid works well. It is escape-proof and keeps out drafts, and you can easily observe your hedgehog.

Place a heating pad underneath one-half to one-third of the aquarium so that your hedgehog can move away from the heated area if he wants. Put the heat setting on low and place pelleted paper bedding on the floor of the aquarium. Place shredded paper over the top of the pelleted paper for environmental enrichment so your hedgehog can hide and tunnel under the shredded paper. Place some hideaways in the aquarium along with your pet's favorite food, water bottle, and toys.

Euthanasia

Even with the very best care, your hedgehog will eventually develop signs of old age or illness. He will no longer be able to run about and enjoy life as he did when he was younger and healthy. This will be a very sad time for you, because your pet's problems cannot be cured and he may be suffering. Eventually you will ask yourself if your pet should be euthanized. When you come to that point, it's the right time to ask your veterinarian for help and guidance.

Euthanasia means putting an animal to death humanely, peacefully, and painlessly. Euthanasia is usually done by first giving the hedgehog a sedative to induce unconsciousness. When the pet can no longer feel pain, an injection of a lethal drug is given that ends his life almost instantly.

Your veterinarian can answer any questions you or your family may have. Your veterinarian can also help you if you wish to find a pet cemetery, have your hedgehog cremated, or have him necropsied.

During this emotional time, take good care of yourself and take time to grieve. Take comfort in the knowledge that you gave your hedgehog the best care possible throughout his life and let happy memories of your little companion replace your sorrow.

Necropsy

Necropsy is the study of body tissues after an animal dies to learn more about the cause of death. Necropsies give us information about health problems and often help us learn how to treat or cure the problem in other animals.

It is understandably a very difficult thing to do, but if your hedgehog dies, or if you must have him euthanized, you may want to think about having your pet necropsied. You and your veterinarian could learn more about your pet's condition, and that information could be passed on and be beneficial in teaching veterinarians how to better help hedgehogs in the future.

Hedgehog Health Chart

Contact your veterinarian right away if your hedgehog has these or any other problems.

Health Problem	Signs
Bite wounds	Sores; lumps; puncture wounds; redness; swelling; bleeding; infection; pus; pain; tenderness
Cancer	Lack of appetite; weight loss; depression; lethargy; inactivity; reclusive; may have visible lumps or masses
Constipation	Straining to pass hard, dry feces; depression; lethargy; lack of appetite
Cardiomyopathy (heart disease)	Lethargy; weight loss; poor condition
Dehydration	Lethargy; weakness; skin tenting; dull eyes
Dental problems	Lack of appetite; drooling; foul odor; tartar accumulation; red or swollen gums; bleeding from mouth; swollen jaws; pain
Diarrhea	Soft, mucous, or liquid feces; foul odor; may have green color; irritation around anus; dehydration, lack of appetite; weight loss; lethargy
Ear disease	Scratching; head shaking; pain; loss of hearing; loss of balance; excessive dander; mites visible around the ears, at the base of the quills, and the quill-less areas of the head. Ears can become encrusted and deformed, ear infections can develop (otitis), and ear canals can be plugged with debris, resulting in hearing loss.
Eye problems	Discharge (runny or matted eyes); eyes partially closed; eye out of eye socket

Causes	What to Do
Animal attacks, fighting	Cleanse wound with gentle antiseptic or antibacterial soap; keep clean; allow to drain; isolate from other animals.
Common in hedgehogs; wide variety of causes, including retroviruses and aging; 65 to 85 percent of hedgehog cases occur in animals more than 3 years of age and are malignant	Keep pet comfortable; seek veterinary treatment; surgery may be helpful.
Not drinking enough; warm, dry environment; dehydration; internal parasites; gastrointestinal obstruction; diseases	Identify cause of problem; encourage drinking.
Many causes and common in hedgehogs	Let your hedgehog rest and avoid stress.
Exposure to hot, dry environment; lack of water; bacterial or viral infections and diseases; stress; heatstroke; vomiting; diarrhea	Encourage drinking.
Excessive tartar accumulation; infection; trauma; cancer of the jaw	Give preventive care by swabbing the teeth with a pet toothpaste, if possible.
Many causes, including internal parasites, bacterial or viral infections, stress, incorrect diet, toxins	Encourage drinking; allow time to recover; wash hands thoroughly after handling.
Mites (*Chorioptes* and *Notoedres* species, and *Caparinia tripilis*); infections; trauma	Gently clean ears; thoroughly clean the hedgehog's housing and accessories; discard all bedding material; change new bedding daily. Obtain veterinary care, as problem can lead to severe quill loss, ear deformation, and hearing loss.
Infection; injury; irritating substances; foreign body; disease. Protruding eye (proptosis) may be caused by trauma or possibly large amounts of fat in the eye socket.	Place in quiet, dark area; if discharge or foreign object is irritating eyes, gently rinse eyes with gentle eyewash solution.

Hedgehog Health Chart (continued)

Health Problem	Signs
Fatty liver disease (hepatic lipidosis)	Lethargy; weakness; lack of appetite; weight loss; death
Heatstroke	Hot; weak; unresponsive; comatose; lying outstretched
Infections	Symptoms vary and include lack of appetite, lethargy, weight loss.
Injury	Pain; anorexia; lethargy; inability to walk or move normally; bleeding; swelling; broken bones
Kidney disease	Excessive drinking and urination; lethargy; dehydration; weight loss
Neurological problems	
Vestibular disease	Lack of coordination; falling over; dizziness; nausea; head tilt; rolling over; nystagmus
Wobbly Hedgehog Syndrome (WHS)	Lack of coordination muscle atrophy; stumbling; falling; difficulty swallowing; tremors; seizures; weight loss; may have protrusion of eye; paralysis; death
Respiratory problems; Pneumonia	Difficulty breathing; snuffling; wheezing; sneezing; discharge from eyes or nose; anorexia; lethargy; weight loss
Skin problems and quill loss	Dry, flaky, scaly skin; excessive dander; red, cracked skin; visible parasites; excessive quill loss; broken quills; bald patches
Urogenital disease	Bloody discharge visible at opening to urinary tract (urethra), or vaginal bleeding

Causes	What to Do
Caused initially by obesity, which leads to excess fat in the liver and abnormal liver function	Take your hedgehog to your veterinarian. Gradually lower fat content in the diet and increase dietary fiber.
Exposure to high temperature; insufficient ventilation	Remove from hot area, hold in hands and submerge body in cool water, keep head above water; when conscious give water.
Bacteria; viruses; fungi; protozoa	Isolate from other animals; wash hands after handling; consult veterinarian
Numerous possibilities, including being bitten, dropped, stepped on, crushed, and burned	Isolate in a quiet, dark area; give first aid treatment
Multiple causes	Make sure water is available at all times and encourage drinking. Give supportive care.
Various causes, including middle-ear infection, tumors, trauma, brain disease	Give supportive care; keep warm and comfortable; encourage eating and drinking; feed with eyedropper or syringe when necessary.
Cause uncertain; believed to be hereditary	Give supportive care; keep warm and comfortable; encourage eating and drinking; feed with eyedropper or syringe when necessary.
Bacterial (*Bordetella*, bronchiseptica, *Pasteurella multocida*), *Mycoplasma*, viral (Cytomegalovirus); fungal; exposure to cold; inhalation of fine dusts; allergies	Keep warm and comfortable; encourage eating and drinking.
Mites (*Caparinia*, *Chorioptes*, and *Sarcoptes*); fleas and flea allergy dermatitis; ticks; bacteria; fungi (*Trichophyton mentagrophytes* var. *erinacei*— "ringworm"); *Arthrodermia benhamiae* and *Microsporum*; improper diet; allergies; cancer; other diseases	Keep hedgehog and cage clean and dry; check for parasites; change bedding often.
Common and may indicate urinary tract infection, cancer, or uterine bleeding	Keep comfortable and encourage eating and drinking.

Hedgehogs keep themselves clean, but during their explorations, they can still get dirty! They are low to the ground, and as they wander about, they come in contact with dust, dirt, and debris. In addition, hedgehogs' anting behavior leaves sticky, dried saliva on their quills that can accumulate shavings, dust, and particulate matter.

Grooming your hedgehog can be a challenging endeavor. It can also be a lot of fun! Every hedgehog is different. Some hedgehogs enjoy grooming and others do not. Some fully cooperate with baths, nail trimming, and even a little dental cleaning. Others curl into a tight ball in protest. Hedgehogs do not need to be groomed often. Once every 3 to 6 months is enough for most hedgehogs.

If you handle your hedgehog frequently and gently on a daily basis, he will be easier to manage when it's time to groom. Grooming may have to take place in several short sessions, especially if your hedgehog becomes upset or stressed, curls into a ball, or struggles to get away from you. For example, you might have to trim your pet's front nails one day and the back nails the following day, and give him a bath on the third day.

Grooming should be enjoyable for both you and your hedgehog. You can make grooming more enjoyable for your hedgehog by talking to him in a soothing voice while you groom him and by offering him tiny food treat rewards during the grooming session.

You will need a few basic and inexpensive supplies to get the job done well!

✔ Spray bottle containing warm water
✔ Gentle hypoallergenic shampoo (do not use shampoos with pesticides) or gentle emollient (nonsoap, such as Allergroom, available from your veterinarian). Use a shampoo or emollient that does not have added scents or fragrances.
✔ Rinsing cup or small sprayer faucet attachment
✔ Small, soft toothbrush
✔ Cotton swabs
✔ Soft cotton towels
✔ Small nail trimmers
✔ Tweezers or small forceps
✔ Pet toothpaste (specifically poultry-flavored CET brand pet toothpaste)
✔ Styptic powder or styptic pencil (a yellow clotting powder commercially available from your pet store or veterinarian)
✔ Penlight
✔ Small washbasin or sink
✔ Aquarium (20 gallon [76 L])
✔ Heating pad
✔ Tiny mealworms or other tasty food morsels for treats

Nail Trimming

Hedgehogs are housed on soft bedding, so they do not have much opportunity to wear their nails down. If the nails grow too long, they can snag on something, tear, and

bleed. Overgrown nails can interfere with your pet's movement and hinder his ability to walk comfortably.

Small nail clippers designed for human babies work well for tiny hedgehog nails. Hedgehogs wear down their nails unevenly, so some nails may need to be trimmed more than others.

Before you trim your pet's nails, gently clean his feet and toes with a clean, damp cloth.

Use a penlight to illuminate the nails to find the line of demarcation where the blood supply (the "quick") ends. Hold your hedgehog's limbs firmly, but gently, so you can carefully trim just the tips of the nails. Don't squeeze or pull on your pet's feet and limbs.

If you accidentally trim the nail too close, apply a small amount of styptic powder or use a styptic stick to stop the bleeding.

Note: The second nail on each hind foot is longer than the other nails. This is normal. Do not trim the nail too close to the nail bed!

Teeth Cleaning

If your hedgehog will let you check his teeth and mouth, you might also be able to gently clean his teeth. Apply a tiny amount of poultry-flavored CET brand toothpaste to a cotton swab and gently dab it on your pet's teeth. Don't be disappointed if your hedgehog won't let you clean his teeth. You can still take this opportunity to check to be sure there are no obvious dental problems. If your hedgehog objects to your cleaning efforts, but needs dental cleaning, your veterinarian can provide that service.

Bathing

With small forceps or tweezers, remove shavings and debris from between your hedgehog's quills.

Place your pet in a small basin, sink, or container. Using the spray bottle, spray warm water on the quills and gently clean the skin and quills with shampoo and a soft toothbrush. The water level in the basin can be up to 1 inch (2.5 cm) deep so your pet's belly hair, legs, and feet can soak clean.

Thoroughly rinse the skin and quills by pouring tepid water from a cup over your pet. Or, if you have a small, gentle sprayer attached to a faucet, turn the water on low and rinse your hedgehog with the sprayer. Be very careful not to get water or shampoo in your hedgehog's eyes, ears, nose, or mouth.

Dry Thoroughly

Dry your hedgehog very well with a warm towel. Gently dry the outside of the ears with a soft cotton swab. Do not push the swab into the ear canal!

Place your hedgehog in a draft-free enclosure, such as a 30-gallon (115 L) Plexiglas aquarium. Do not let him get chilled. Place a heating pad, on low setting, under one half of the aquarium, so your hedgehog can use, or avoid, the heat source as needed.

When your hedgehog is completely dry and warm, he can be returned to his usual enclosure.

RAISING AFRICAN PYGMY HEDGEHOGS

It's a huge leap from the joys of caring for a single hedgehog to the challenges and responsibilities of raising them! Before you undertake this fascinating and demanding hobby, you need to have the knowledge, time, finances, and facilities to do it right. There is a lot to know to successfully produce healthy, well-socialized, attractive hedgehog pets.

Why do you want to raise hedgehogs? If your reasons are strictly money driven and you think you can make a profit, you should reconsider. Raising hedgehogs is expensive when you add up the costs of breeding stock, housing, materials, supplies, food, health care, and animal loss.

Raising hedgehogs is not easy. Females can die from pregnancy complications, or require surgery to deliver the babies. Newborn mortality is high. In addition, some hedgehogs carry genetic disorders that may not become apparent until generations later in the breeding program. Finally, breeders must find good homes for every single animal they produce, or keep the animals themselves. Responsible breeders *always* make sure they have loving homes lined up for the babies *before* they breed their animals.

If you want to raise hedgehogs because hedgehogs are your passion and your goals are to produce well-socialized and friendly pets, improve breeding stock, reduce the incidence of inherited health problems, and educate people about these wonderful animals, then welcome to the world of ethical, responsible, reputable hedgehog breeders!

To-Do List for the New Hedgehog Breeder

1. Learn as much as possible about hedgehogs.

2. Check to be sure that hedgehog ownership and breeding is legal in your state and area.

3. Study the Animal Welfare Act (see "Information"). The United States Department of Agriculture (USDA) requires that hedgehog breeders comply with it.

4. Fill out the USDA Plan of Veterinary Care form. USDA veterinary inspectors check hedge-hog-breeding facilities annually for compliance with USDA regulations.

5. Obtain a USDA license: Class A for breeders, Class B for brokers. Licensure is required by federal law of anyone who raises, sells, or gives away African pygmy hedgehogs.

6. Keep current on which states allow you to sell and ship hedgehogs. Regulations change periodically.

7. If you plan to ship hedgehogs by air (not recommended), find out which airlines in your state will transport them according to USDA and Animal Welfare Act regulations.

8. Write your health guarantees, contracts, sales policies, and information pamphlets. Include a written policy saying that you will take back hedgehogs that you sell that don't work out for the buyers.

9. Plan your marketing and advertising: develop a website, place ads in pet magazines.

10. Choose a veterinarian.

11. Select and purchase breeding stock.

12. Register your animals with the appropriate hedgehog registries.

13. Develop a detailed record-keeping system for all of your animals.

14. Join a hedgehog club, attend educational seminars, and participate in hedgehog shows.

15. Learn about genetics and the different hedgehog lines. Find out which lineages have the best health and temperament.

16. Have an emergency preparedness plan in place, including a method for animal evacuation in case of disaster (flood, fire, earthquake, hurricanes).

17. Purchase a generator for backup power in case of power failures so you can maintain your hedgehog colony at a comfortable temperature with ventilation and lighting.

Consider how many animals you have time, money, and space to keep. Keep animal numbers reasonable so you can give each hedgehog the excellent care he/she deserves.

✔ Make sure you have homes reserved for baby hedgehogs *before* you breed your animals.

✔ Have a plan for your retired breeders. Hedge-hogs can't spend their entire lives reproducing. At some point, your hedgehogs need to "retire." Do you have space to keep them when they retire or have loving homes lined up for them?

As a hedgehog breeder you will have active breeders, retired breeders, and show animals, plus several babies and younger animals that you will retain to keep your hobby active. You're going to be very busy, indeed!

Hedgehog Reproductive Characteristics

African pygmy hedgehogs are unique and primitive mammals. So it's not surprising that extensive studies of their anatomy, reproductive tracts, and gametes (egg and sperm) reveal that these hedgehogs also have some unique and unusual reproductive characteristics.

Females (Sows)

The female African pygmy hedgehog normally has five pairs of mammary glands (teats): one thoracic pair and four abdominal pairs, located ventro-laterally. (The number of teats can vary.)

The uterus has two "horns" (bicornate). The uterine horns, more accurately called *uterine tubes*, branch from a large, thin-walled vagina.

African Pygmy Hedgehog Reproduction

Breeding season in the wild	January–March
Breeding season in captivity	Year-round
Sexual maturity	As early as 2 months of age for both sexes
Recommended breeding age	6 months to 2½ years for females; many males can be used for breeding throughout their lives
Estrous cycle	Induced ovulator
Gestation	34 to 37 days
Placentation	Chorioallantoic
Litter size	1 to 7 babies (average 3 to 4 babies)
Colostrum production	1 to 3 days postpartum (after giving birth)
Lactation	6 to 8 weeks
Weaning	4 to 8 weeks (weaning is usually complete by 6 weeks, but babies should remain with mother for 8 weeks)
Physical maturity	6 months of age or older

The fallopian tubes are simple in structure compared with most mammals and are extremely short for the hedgehog's size. The ovaries are contained within capsules (bursa).

African pygmy hedgehogs are induced ovulators. This means that mating must occur in order for the ovary to release an egg(s) to be fertilized. Experimentally, African pygmy hedgehogs have been shown to pass six to eight eggs when ovulation is stimulated. This is consistent with their litter sizes, which range from one to seven babies, with an average of three to four.

Males (Boars)

The penis is contained within a sheath, called the prepuce, located approximately mid-abdomen and is sometimes mistaken for a large "belly button" by inexperienced hedgehog owners. When the tip (glans) of the hedgehog penis protrudes from the prepuce, it has a "snail-like" form, with a rounded protrusion on either side of the urethral opening. The hedgehog's penis does not have surface spines, which are commonly found in species closely related to hedgehogs and some other mammals.

The African pygmy hedgehog's testicles are located low in the pelvic area within the abdomen in the para-anal recesses. The testicles usually cannot be felt. There is no scrotum. The epididymis lies in a shallow cremaster sac.

The seminal vesicles are multi-lobed and the prostate gland is bi-lobed. The male has a pair of Cowper's glands. Each gland is on the side of the urethra below the prostate gland. The prostate gland and Cowper's glands secrete fluid into the semen.

An interesting African pygmy hedgehog reproductive trait is the asymmetric insertion of the sperm tail onto the sperm head, which probably accounts for the hedgehog's sperm traveling in a slightly bent position.

Courtship Behavior

Courtship can be a very noisy and aggressive event. Always closely supervise your hedgehogs when you put them together for breeding, to be sure that they do not fight or injure each other.

Start by placing the female in the male's cage. Evenings are a good time to introduce the female to the male, when the animals are most active. Some breeders place more than one female at a time in with a single male for breeding, but it is safer to monitor two animals than several. Hedgehogs can injure their mouths on quills if they quarrel and bite. Check to be sure your pets' mouths are not injured or bleeding.

Courtship usually begins with the male making various noises, sometimes referred to as "serenading" or "singing," and circling the female. The female may initially rebuff the male by raising her quills, snorting, huffing, squeaking, and running away from him. The male may pursue the female more aggressively and nip at her feet and legs. Eventually, if the female is receptive to the male, she will lie flat and allow the male to mount from behind and mate. If the female continues to reject the male, or one or both of the animals act aggressively, the female should be removed from the area and reintroduced later.

The actual mating process is very brief. The breeding ritual may trigger anting behavior.

To prevent possible fighting and injury, the male should be separated from the female shortly after breeding.

The male should never be housed with the mother and babies.

Pregnancy

The female should be housed alone during pregnancy. Pregnancy imposes huge demands on the mother hedgehog, and her caloric requirements increase significantly. She may double or triple her usual food intake, depending on the number of babies she is carrying. She should be allowed to eat as much as she needs.

Pregnancy can be life threatening in some cases, such as when the female is unable to give birth naturally, has a ruptured uterus or difficulty giving birth (dystocia), and needs surgery (Cesarian section). Breeding your female hedgehog should not be taken lightly. If your hedgehog is less than six months, or more than three years of age, she should not be bred.

Pregnancy can be difficult to detect in African pygmy hedgehogs, and is usually diagnosed by weight gain, so be sure to weigh your female weekly and record her weights and breeding date.

Females can gain 40 to 50 g by the time they are three to four weeks into their pregnancy. Pregnant females usually show teat and mammary gland enlargement as they near parturition (the delivery date).

False pregnancy is common in African pygmy hedgehogs and fetal resorption is also possible.

Litter size is determined by the number of viable eggs the female ovulates and the number of viable sperm the male provides during copulation.

Handle your female gently and with care, and do not disturb her more than necessary. Give her a spacious enclosure with pelleted paper bedding and several hideaways. One month after breeding takes place, give her enclosure a final, thorough cleaning before the babies are born; then do not disturb her at all. Spot cleaning and feeding should be done quietly while the mother is sleeping.

A few days before giving birth, the female will remain hidden in her hideaway. She may push bedding around to block the entry to the hideaway or nest box where she will give birth. It is common for the female to stop eating, or eat less, one to two days before delivery.

Birth (Partuition)

Hedgehogs usually give birth at night. Shortly before giving birth, at the onset of labor, the female will become extremely active. During partuition, the mother hedgehog clears away the placenta, blood, fluids, and membranes, and

African Pygmy Hedgehog Growth and Development

Age	Male	Female	Comment
Birth	13 g	9 g	Weight ranges 4.5 to 13 g. Runts (4.5 to 6.5 g) seldom survive. Newborns 9 g or more have a greater chance of survival. Flat, soft, white quills can be seen beneath swollen skin surface.
1 to 2 hours			First quills emerge.
24 hours			Second set of darker quills emerge. Skin and nose begin to pigment (darken).
2 to 3 days			Second set of quills begin to emerge.
10 days	120 g	80 g	Weight ranges 40 to 130 g; varies with individuals. Rapid weight gain in first 10 days of life.
10 to 14 days			Able to roll into a partial ball.
18 days (range 14 to 24 days)			Eyes and ears begin to open. Hair begins to grow.
15 days	Anting (self-anointing) behavior	Anting (self-anointing) behavior	Babies may lick mother's quills and then "self-anoint".
21 days			Teeth begin to erupt. Babies start to explore environment.
4 weeks			Able to roll into a tight ball.
4 to 6 weeks			Weaning begins.
6 to 7 weeks	Separate males from female siblings and mother		Separate males from all females to prevent accidental matings and unwanted pregnancies.
6 to 8 weeks			Babies weaned (some babies will suckle up to 12 weeks or more if they are not separated from their mothers).
10 to 12 weeks	Separate males from each other		Separate males to prevent fighting.

African Pygmy Hedgehog Growth and Development (continued)

Age	Male	Female	Comment
12 weeks			Babies can go to new homes.
3 to 6 months	450–600 g	315–450 g	Adult size obtained. Some hedgehogs have temperament (behavior) changes that may be related to hormonal influences as they reach puberty (sexual maturity).
Adult	16–21 oz. 448–588 g 500 g average	8–18 oz. 224–504 g 380 g average	

cleans her babies. She raises her babies alone, without the help of the father.

Mother hedgehogs are highly protective of their young and lunge, head-butt, hiss, and bite at intruders. If the mother is upset or disturbed, she may reject or cannibalize her babies.

Lactation (Milk Production)

Lactation places such great energy demands on the mother hedgehog that her food consumption can increase three times or more. Mother hedgehogs should be fed a high-quality diet, free choice, during this very critical time or she can stop lactating and the babies will starve.

Colostrum is the "first milk" that is secreted during the first one to three days after birth. Its composition is different from that of regular hedgehog milk. It is very important that the babies receive colostrum because it provides temporary immunity against some diseases in the form of immunoglobulins and increases the babies' chances of survival. After colostrum production ceases, the mother produces milk of a different composition to feed her family.

Preventing Stress and Death

✔ Mother hedgehogs with babies should never be disturbed or stressed. Loud sounds, the scent of other animals, and other stressful situations can cause mother hedgehogs to kill and cannibalize their offspring.

✔ Cannibalism is especially common among young or first-time mother hedgehogs.

✔ During the first three weeks after birth, do not clean the cage. Spot-clean only while the mother is sleeping. Be cautious and quiet when you provide food and water.

✔ Mother hedgehogs are stressed by noises and bright lights. They should have lots of hideaways. Their enclosures should be placed in quiet areas with subdued lighting.

✔ Do not house other hedgehogs with the mother and her babies or the babies can be killed and eaten.

✔ Mother hedgehogs may carry their squeaking babies about the cage until they settle into a hiding place they consider safe and secure. Do not interfere with the mother during this time. Allow her to settle down on her own.

Newborns

Baby hedgehogs (hoglets, pups) are born with soft, flexible, white spines that are visible under their delicate, swollen pink skin. Within one to two hours the swelling goes down and the quills emerge and gradually harden. At two days of age a second set of quills emerge that are darker in color and firmer.

Babies are able to crawl and search for nipples. They often suckle on their backs and require very small but frequent meals. Babies will suckle 16 times or more in a 24-hour period.

If one or more pups in the litter die, it may be because they are too weak to suckle properly and are not getting enough milk. If all of the litter is doing poorly, the mother may not be producing enough (or any) milk to support them. Some authors suggest checking to see if the mother is producing milk by gently pressing the teats to see if milk comes out of them. This is not recommended unless absolutely necessary because it requires handling, uncurling, and disturbing the mother.

If your baby hedgehogs do not have enough to eat, you will have to hand-feed them with a syringe (see "Feeding Your Hedgehog").

Sexing Hedgehogs

It's easy to tell the sex of African pygmy hedgehogs by examining the external genitalia. Hold the baby carefully, belly up, with its back against the palm of your hand. Locate the anus, under the tail, and proceed upward to the genital opening. The distance from the anus to the genital opening (ano-genital orifice) is greater in the male. The sheath of the penis is on the abdomen and should not be confused with the umbilical cord in newborns, or with a "belly button" in sexually mature males. In females, the ano-genital distance is very short.

Baby Hedgehog Survival

Conception rates are relatively high in African pygmy hedgehogs. Unfortunately, newborn mortality rates are also high. Some breeders lose as many as one-third of their baby hedgehogs before they are weaned. The first 24 hours of life are the most critical. Most deaths are caused by maternal neglect, cannibalism, hypothermia (being too cold), hypoglycemia (low blood sugar from not receiving enough food), or dehydration. Baby hedgehog death rates are highest in primiparous (first-time) mothers, mothers over

two and a half years of age, and mothers under six months of age. Neglected or orphaned baby hedgehogs are very difficult to care for, and survival rates are low.

THE HEDGEHOG CONNOISSEUR

As a budding hedgehog expert, you know there is no limit to the fun you can have with your African pygmy hedgehog. Now is a great time to take the next step and participate in hedgehog shows, exhibitions, clubs, and educational seminars.

When you tell people you have a pet hedgehog, do they give you a funny look? And do they follow up by asking you a lot of questions about your pet? If so, it's time to educate your friends and show others what a fascinating and charismatic animal your precious pygmy hedgehog is! One of the best ways to promote your pet is by playing an active role in hedgehog clubs, shows, activities, and informational seminars.

Colorful Quills, Clubs, and Shows

Just like people, every hedgehog differs in personality and appearance. African pygmy hedgehogs come in a wide variety of colorful quills. In fact, at this time the International Hedgehog Association recognizes 92 variations of quill coloration.

Genetic color inheritance of the skin, quills, and eyes is a very complicated subject that goes beyond the scope of this hedgehog manual. The exact genetic inheritance for each possible hedgehog color has not yet been completely determined, but hedgehog breeders are making great progress by keeping accurate records and sharing their information.

In any breeding program, the animal's health, temperament, and conformation are the most important factors. Color is important, but it should always be a secondary consideration. In other words, an African pygmy hedgehog's health and personality are more important than his color.

Information about hedgehog show standards, scheduled hedgehog shows and events, and hedgehog color types, patterns, and varieties can be found on the International Hedgehog Association website. The International Hedgehog Association also maintains an active hedgehog registry (see "Information").

Your hedgehog may simply be a home companion, but if you think he's handsome enough to compete against the very best, give it a try! You'll have a lot of fun, you'll learn a lot, and you'll make friends, too! So make some room on that shelf, because who knows? It just might be your pet's turn to bring home the trophy!

Travel with Your Hedgehog

Traveling with your hedgehog is easy. Pet stores sell a wide variety of small travel kennels made of smooth plastic that are suitable for hedgehogs. These kennels are safe, lightweight, easy to clean, and well ventilated, and have doors that latch securely.

Whether you are going to a hedgehog show, taking a vacation, or transporting your pet to the veterinarian, your hedgehog will travel more comfortably if he has had a chance to get used

to the travel kennel before you take him on a trip. To do this, remove the door to the travel kennel, place a food treat and a hideaway inside, and give your hedgehog time to explore the travel kennel.

During travel, your hedgehog needs space to stand and turn around comfortably. Take a water dish and bottled water for the trip (water bottles tend to leak during travel) and food. Reduce noise and light as much as possible. Cover the travel kennel to reduce sounds and light, but be sure there is plenty of ventilation.

Never leave your hedgehog in the car if the weather is warm; your pet could die of heatstroke.

Travel by air is not recommended for your hedgehog, unless absolutely necessary. The loud noises and air-conditioning can stress your pet.

Be sure to check with the airlines to see if they allow hedgehogs and if you can reserve a space for your pet to travel with you in the cabin. If your hedgehog must travel in the cargo area, it is better to leave him at home with a pet sitter. But if you absolutely must take him with you, make sure that there is cargo space designated for animal transport, so that it is pressurized and temperature con- trolled, and give your hedgehog plenty of extra bedding material to help him keep warm.

Check with airlines for their most recent reg- ulations. At this time, airlines require the pet owner to obtain an interstate health certificate from a USDA-accredited veterinarian that says the animal has been examined and is healthy enough to travel.

✔ *The veterinary health certificate must be dated not more than 10 days before the day of travel.*

✔ *Hedgehogs should not be vaccinated.*

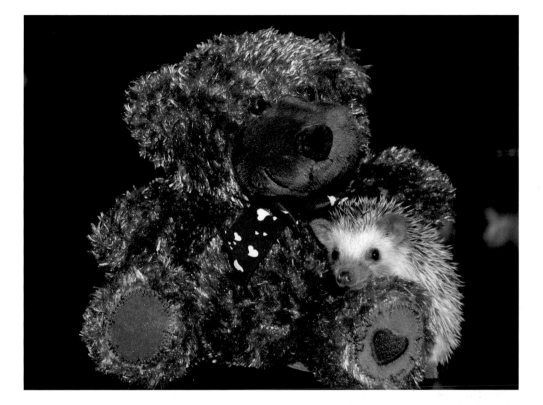

✔ *Do not give your hedgehog tranquilizers or sedatives for travel. These can cause death at high altitudes.*

Head Over Heels About Hedgehogs!

African pygmy hedgehogs have proven themselves to be extraordinary pets. Inquisitive and cute, they have brought friendship, entertainment, and happiness to thousands. From the vast wild continent of Africa, to recognition in ancient literature and art—to research laboratories, and finally into your loving home—the African pygmy hedgehog is a world traveler *and* a time traveler. They have come a long way and changed little from the primitive era of the birth of their species. We have solved some of our hedgehogs' mysteries, but most remain unanswered. The secretive hedgehog is a charming enigma that deserves his growing status today as an adored pet.

So the next time you hold your hedgehog and look into his bright eyes and find yourself helplessly smitten, remember there are countless other hedgehog aficionados who feel the same way about their hedgehog as you do. You're in good company!

INFORMATION

Organizations

American Association of Zoo Veterinarians
581705 White Oak Road
Yulee, FL 32097
(904) 225-3275
E-mail: aazvorg@aol.com
www.aazv.org

American Society of Mammologists
P.O. Box 1897
Lawrence, KS 66044
(785) 843-1235
(800) 627-0326
www.mammalsociety.org

American Veterinary Medical Association
1931 N. Meacham Road, Suite 100
Schaumberg, IL 60173-4360
(847) 925-8070
E-mail: avmainfo@avma.org
www.avma.org

Association of Exotic Mammal Veterinarians
P.O. Box 396
Weare, NH 03281-0396
Fax: (478) 757-1315
E-mail: info@aemv.org
www.aema.org

International Hedgehog Association
P.O. Box 1060
Divide, CO 80814
E-mail: info@hedgehogclub.com
http://hedgehogclub.com

United States Department of Agriculture
Animal and Plant Health Inspection Services
www.aphis.usda.gov

Magazines

*Critters USA Annual Guide to Caring for
    Exotic Mammals*
Irvine, CA: Fancy Publications
(949) 855-8822
www.animalnetwork.com

Journal of Exotic Pet Medicine
Elsevier Saunders
www.exoticpetmedicine.com

Books

Johnson-Delaney, Cathy. *Exotic Companion
    Medicine Handbook.* Lake Worth, FL: Wingers
    Publishing, 1996.
Kelsey-Wood, D. *The Cult of the Hedgehog.*
    Neptune, NJ: TFH Publications, 1997.
Nowak, Ronald, ed. *Walker's Mammals of the
    World.* Baltimore and London: The Johns
    Hopkins University Press, 1999.
Quessenberry, K. E., and E. V. Hillyer. *The Veteri-
    nary Clinics of North America, Small Animal
    Practice, Exotic Pet Medicine II,* Vol. 24, No. 1.
    Philadelphia, PA: W.B. Saunders Company,
    1994.
Reeve, Nigel. *Hedgehogs.* San Diego, CA:
    Academic Press, 1996.
Wrobel, D. *The Hedgehog.* Hoboken, NJ: Wiley
    Publishing, 2002.

INDEX

About the Author

Sharon Vanderlip, DVM, has a Bachelor of Science degree in zoology from the University of California at Davis and a degree in veterinary medicine. Dr. Vanderlip has provided veterinary care to exotic, wild, and domestic animals for more than 30 years. She has published in scientific journals and has authored more than 20 books on pet care. Dr. Vanderlip owns a specialty practice, has served as clinical veterinarian for the University of California at San Diego School of Medicine, has collaborated on research projects with the San Diego Zoo, and is former chief of veterinary services for the National Aeronautics and Space Administration. Dr. Vanderlip has kept African pygmy and European hedgehogs as pets and has cared for numerous hedgehogs in her practice. She may be contacted for seminars at *www.sharonvanderlip.com.*

Acknowledgments

A big thank-you to my husband, Jack Vanderlip, DVM, for sharing his expertise in laboratory and exotic animal medicine, for his critical review of the final manuscript, and for helping at home and in our practice so I could have time to research and write this book. Thanks to our daughter, Jacquelynn, for her help and photos. Finally, thanks to everyone at Pet Kingdom in Las Vegas, Nevada, for their hospitality and enthusiasm.

Important Note

Many pet owners feel that the pronoun "it" is not appropriate when referring to a pet that can be such a wonderful part of our lives. For those instances in this book where a specific pet hedgehog is described, the pronoun "he" is used. However when talking about hedgehogs in general, the pronoun "it" has been used. The use of "he" by no means infers any preference, nor should it be taken as an indication that either sex is particularly problematic.

Cover Photos

Deneen Foelker: front cover; Jacquelynn Vanderlip: back cover, inside back cover; Kimberly Goertzen: inside front cover.

Photo Credits

Deneen Foelker: pages 91 (top and bottom), 95 (bottom); Kimberly Goertzen: pages 2–3, 4, 11, 18, 48, 49, 58, 73, 84, 86, 93, 94, 95 (top), 96; Jacquelynn Vanderlip: pages 5, 7, 8, 9, 14, 15, 16, 19, 21, 22, 25, 26 (left and right), 28, 29, 30 (top and bottom), 31, 33 (top and bottom), 36, 37, 38, 41, 44, 45 (top and bottom), 46, 47, 50, 51, 52, 53, 54, 55, 57, 64, 65, 68, 70, 74, 78, 79, 85, 87, 97, 98, 101; Jill Warnick: pages 27, 32, 63, 77, 99.

© Copyright 2010 by Barron's Educational Series, Inc.

All rights reserved.
No part of this book may be reproduced or distributed in any form or by any other means without the written permission of the copyright owner.

All inquiries should be addressed to:
Barron's Educational Series, Inc.
250 Wireless Boulevard
Hauppauge, NY 11788
www.barronseduc.com

ISBN-13: 978-0-7641-4439-4
ISBN-10: 0-7641-4439-1

Library of Congress Catalog Card No. 2009050636

Library of Congress Cataloging-in-Publication Data
Vanderlip, Sharon Lynn.
    Hedgehogs/ Sharon L. Vanderlip.
        p. cm. — (A complete pet owner's manual)
    Includes bibliographical references and index.
    ISBN-13: 978-0-7641-4439-4 (alk. paper)
    ISBN-10: 0-7641-4439-1 (alk. paper)
    1. Hedgehogs. I. Title.
    SF459.H43V36 2010
    636.933'2—dc22   2009050636

Printed in China
9 8 7 6